_To_

---

_From_

---

_Date_

*God's Promises for Your Every Need*
Copyright © 2006 Thomas Nelson

Published in Nashville, Tennessee, by Thomas Nelson. Thomas
Nelson is a registered trademark of HarperCollins Christian
Publishing, Inc.

Scripture quotations are from the New King James Version®. © 1982
by Thomas Nelson. Used by permission. All rights reserved.

Compiled by Dr. A. L. Gill.

ISBN: 978-0-529-10080-1

Library of Congress Cataloging-in-Publication Data
    Bible. English. Authorized. Selections. 2006.
    God's promises for your every need / [compiled by A.L. Gill].
       p. cm.
    ISBN: 1-4041-0410-0 (25th Anniversary edition, softcover)
    ISBN: 1-4041-0411-9 (25th Anniversary edition, leather)
    1. God—Promises—Biblical teaching. 2. Bible—Use.
  I. Gill, A. L. II. Title.
    BS680.P68B53 2006
    220.5'208—dc22

2006000935

*Printed in China*

23 24 25 26 27 GRI 21 20 19 18 17

# GOD'S
# PROMISES®
## *for Your*
# EVERY
# NEED

## NKJV

An Imprint of Thomas Nelson Publishers

THOMAS NELSON
*Since 1798*

# CONTENTS

# JESUS
# IS
# YOUR . . .

JESUS IS YOUR . . .

# SAVIOR

Not by works of righteousness which we have done, but according to His mercy He saved us, through the washing of regeneration and renewing of the Holy Spirit, whom He poured out on us abundantly through Jesus Christ our Savior.

TITUS 3:5–6

For by grace you have been saved through faith, and that not of yourselves; it is the gift of God, not of works, lest anyone should boast.

EPHESIANS 2:8–9

And we have seen and testify that the Father has sent the Son as Savior of the world.

1 JOHN 4:14

For we ourselves have heard Him and we know that this is indeed the Christ, the Savior of the world.

JOHN 4:42

For the Son of Man has come to seek and to save that which was lost.

LUKE 19:10

Being justified freely by His grace through the redemption that is in Christ Jesus, whom God set forth as a propitiation by His blood, through faith, to demonstrate His righteousness, because in His forbearance God had passed over the sins that were previously committed.

ROMANS 3:24–25

But God, who is rich in mercy, because of His great love with which He loved us, even when we were dead in trespasses, made us alive together with Christ (by grace you have been saved).

EPHESIANS 2:4–5

That if you confess with your mouth the Lord Jesus and believe in your heart that God has raised Him from the dead, you will be saved.

ROMANS 10:9

And my spirit has rejoiced in God my Savior.

LUKE 1:47

Most assuredly, I say to you, he who believes in Me has everlasting life.

JOHN 6:47

For God so loved the world that He gave His only begotten Son, that whoever believes in Him should not perish but have everlasting life.

JOHN 3:16

Who has saved us and called us with a holy calling, not according to our works, but according to His own purpose and grace which was given to us in Christ Jesus before time began.

2 TIMOTHY 1:9

Therefore, if anyone is in Christ, he is a new creation; old things have passed away; behold, all things have become new.

2 CORINTHIANS 5:17

Nevertheless He saved them for His name's sake, That He might make His mighty power known.

PSALM 106:8

JESUS IS YOUR . . .

# LORD

---

Therefore God also has highly exalted Him and given Him the name which is above every name, that at the name of Jesus every knee should bow, of those in heaven, and of those on earth, and of those under the earth, and that every tongue should confess that Jesus Christ is Lord, to the glory of God the Father.

PHILIPPIANS 2:9–11

That if you confess with your mouth the Lord Jesus and believe in your heart that God has raised him from the dead, you will be saved. For with the heart one believes unto righteousness, and with the mouth confession is made unto salvation.

ROMANS 10:9–10

But why do you call Me "Lord, Lord," and not do the things which I say?

LUKE 6:46

For sin shall not have dominion over you, for you are not under law but under grace.

What then? Shall we sin because we are not under law but under grace? Certainly not! Do you not know that to whom you present yourselves slaves to obey, you are that one's slaves whom you obey, whether of sin leading to death, or of obedience leading to righteousness?

ROMANS 6:14–16

I beseech you therefore, brethren, by the mercies of God, that you present your bodies a living sacrifice, holy, acceptable to God, which is your reasonable service. And do not be conformed to this world, but be transformed by the renewing of your mind, that you may prove what is that good and acceptable and perfect will of God.

ROMANS 12:1–2

Therefore let all the house of Israel know assuredly that God has made this Jesus, whom you crucified, both Lord and Christ.

ACTS 2:36

Or do you not know that your body is the temple of the Holy Spirit who is in you, whom you have from God, and you are not your own? For you were bought at a price; therefore glorify God in your body and in your spirit, which are God's.

1 CORINTHIANS 6:19–20

For if we live, we live to the Lord; and if we die, we die to the Lord. Therefore, whether we live or die, we are the Lord's.

ROMANS 14:8

Blessed be the Lord,
    Who daily loads us with benefits,
    The God of our salvation! Selah

PSALM 68:19

For the Lord GOD will help me;
    Therefore I will not be disgraced;
    Therefore I have set My face like a flint,
    And I know that I will not be ashamed.

ISAIAH 50:7

For You, Lord, are good, and ready to forgive,
And abundant in mercy to all those who call
upon You.

PSALM 86:5

And you shall love the L<small>ORD</small> your God with all your heart, with all your soul, with all your mind, and with all your strength. This is the first commandment.

MARK 12:30

But it is good for me to draw near to God;
I have put my trust in the Lord G<small>OD</small>,
That I may declare all Your works.

PSALM 73:28

For David says concerning him:
"I foresaw the L<small>ORD</small> always before my face,
For He is at my right hand, that I may not be
shaken."

ACTS 2:25

JESUS IS YOUR . . .

# LOVE

But God demonstrates His own love toward us, in that while we were still sinners, Christ died for us.

ROMANS 5:8

The LORD has appeared of old to me, saying:
"Yes, I have loved you with an everlasting love;
Therefore with lovingkindness I have drawn you."

JEREMIAH 31:3

I love those who love me,
And those who seek me diligently will find me.

PROVERBS 8:17

And we have known and believed the love that God has for us. God is love, and he who abides in love abides in God, and God in him. . . .
We love Him because He first loved us.

1 JOHN 4:16, 19

Beloved, let us love one another, for love is of God; and everyone who loves is born of God and knows God. He who does not love does not know God, for God is love. In this the love of God was manifested toward us, that God has sent his only begotten Son into the world, that we might live through Him. In this is love, not that we loved God, but that He loved us and sent His Son to be the propitiation for our sins. Beloved, if God so loved us, we also ought to love one another.

No one has seen God at any time. If we love one another, God abides in us, and His love has been perfected in us.

1 JOHN 4:7–12

He who has My commandments and keeps them, it is he who loves Me. And he who loves Me will be loved by My Father, and I will love him and manifest Myself to him.

JOHN 14:21

And now abide faith, hope, love, these three; but the greatest of these is love.

1 CORINTHIANS 13:13

That Christ may dwell in your hearts through faith; that you, being rooted and grounded in love, may be able to comprehend with all the saints what is the width and length and depth and height—to know the love of Christ which passes knowledge; that you may be filled with all the fullness of God.

EPHESIANS 3:17–19

I will betroth you to Me forever;
  Yes, I will betroth you to Me
  In righteousness and justice,
  In lovingkindness and mercy.

HOSEA 2:19

For God so loved the world that He gave His only begotten Son, that whoever believes in Him should not perish but have everlasting life.

JOHN 3:16

The Lord will command His lovingkindness in the daytime,
  And in the night His song shall be with me—
  A prayer to the God of my life.

PSALM 42:8

As the Father loved Me, I also have loved you; abide in My love. If you keep My commandments, you will abide in My love, just as I have kept My Father's commandments and abide in His love.

These things I have spoken to you, that My joy may remain in you, and that your joy may be full. This is My commandment, that you love one another as I have loved you. Greater love has no one than this, than to lay down one's life for his friends. . . .

These things I command you, that you love one another.

JOHN 15:9–13, 17

For I am persuaded that neither death nor life, nor angels nor principalities nor powers, nor things present nor things to come, nor height nor depth, nor any other created thing, shall be able to separate us from the love of God which is in Christ Jesus our Lord.

ROMANS 8:38–39

JESUS IS YOUR . . .

# PEACE

You will keep him in perfect peace,
  Whose mind is stayed on You,
  Because he trusts in You.

ISAIAH 26:3

But now in Christ Jesus you who once were far off
have been brought near by the blood of Christ.

For He Himself is our peace, who has made
both one, and has broken down the middle wall of
separation.

EPHESIANS 2:13–14

LORD, You will establish peace for us,
  For You have also done all our works in us.

ISAIAH 26:12

The things which you learned and received and
heard and saw in me, these do, and the God of
peace will be with you.

PHILIPPIANS 4:9

Therefore, having been justified by faith, we have peace with God through our Lord Jesus Christ.

ROMANS 5:1

Be anxious for nothing, but in everything by prayer and supplication, with thanksgiving, let your requests be made known to God; and the peace of God, which surpasses all understanding, will guard your hearts and minds through Christ Jesus.

PHILIPPIANS 4:6–7

And let the peace of God rule in your hearts, to which also you were called in one body; and be thankful.

COLOSSIANS 3:15

The LORD will give strength to His people;
The LORD will bless His people with peace.

PSALM 29:11

And the God of peace will crush Satan under your feet shortly.
The grace of our Lord Jesus Christ be with you. Amen.

ROMANS 16:20

For unto us a Child is born,
Unto us a Son is given;
And the government will be upon His shoulder.
And His name will be called
Wonderful, Counselor, Mighty God,
Everlasting Father, Prince of Peace.
Of the increase of His government and peace
There will be no end,
Upon the throne of David and over His kingdom,
To order it and establish it with judgment and
justice
From that time forward, even forever.
The zeal of the LORD of hosts will perform this.

ISAIAH 9:6–7

I will both lie down in peace, and sleep;
For You alone, O LORD, make me dwell in safety.

PSALM 4:8

Peace I leave with you, My peace I give to you; not as the world gives do I give to you. Let not your heart be troubled, neither let it be afraid.

JOHN 14:27

JESUS IS YOUR . . .

# FORGIVENESS

---

To the praise of the glory of His grace, by which He made us accepted in the Beloved.

In Him we have redemption through His blood, the forgiveness of sins, according to the riches of His grace.

EPHESIANS 1:6–7

Let the wicked forsake his way,
 And the unrighteous man his thoughts?
 Let him return to the Lord,
 And He will have mercy on him;
 And to our God,
 For He will abundantly pardon.

ISAIAH 55:7

I will cleanse them from all their iniquity by which they have sinned against Me, and I will pardon all their iniquities by which they have sinned and by which they have transgressed against Me.

JEREMIAH 33:8

You have forgiven the iniquity of Your people;
    You have covered all their sin. Selah

Therefore, if anyone is in Christ, he is a new creation; old things have passed away; behold, all things have become new.

2 CORINTHIANS 5:17

As far as the east is from the west,
    So far has He removed our transgressions
        from us.

PSALM 103:12

My little children, these things I write to you, so that you may not sin. And if anyone sins, we have an Advocate with the Father, Jesus Christ the righteous.

1 JOHN 2:1

Bearing with one another, and forgiving one another, if anyone has a complaint against another; even as Christ forgave you, so you also must do.

COLOSSIANS 3:13

If we confess our sins, He is faithful and just to forgive us our sins and to cleanse us from all unrighteousness.

1 JOHN 1:9

For I will be merciful to their unrighteousness, and their sins and their lawless deeds I will remember no more.

HEBREWS 8:12

And whenever you stand praying, if you have anything against anyone, forgive him, that your Father in heaven may also forgive you your trespasses.

MARK 11:25

"Come now, and let us reason together,"
    Says the LORD,
    "Though your sins are like scarlet,
    They shall be as white as snow;
    Though they are red like crimson,
    They shall be as wool."

ISAIAH 1:18

And you, being dead in your trespasses and the uncircumcision of your flesh, He has made alive together with Him, having forgiven you all trespasses.

COLOSSIANS 2:13

I, even I, am He who blots out your transgressions
for My own sake;
And I will not remember your sins.

ISAIAH 43:25

JESUS IS YOUR . . .

# RIGHTEOUSNESS

For He made Him who knew no sin to be sin for us, that we might become the righteousness of God in Him.

2 CORINTHIANS 5:21

But of Him you are in Christ Jesus, who became for us wisdom from God—and righteousness and sanctification and redemption.

1 CORINTHIANS 1:30

And be found in Him, not having my own righteousness, which is from the law, but that which is through faith in Christ, the righteousness which is from God by faith.

PHILIPPIANS 3:9

Even the righteousness of God, through faith in Jesus Christ, to all and on all who believe. For there is no difference.

ROMANS 3:22

Just as Abraham "believed God, and it was accounted to him for righteousness." Therefore know that only those who are of faith are sons of Abraham.

GALATIANS 3:6–7

Being justified freely by His grace through the redemption that is in Christ Jesus, whom God set forth as a propitiation by His blood, through faith, to demonstrate His righteousness, because in His for-bearance God had passed over the sins that were previously committed, to demonstrate at the present time His righteousness, that He might be just and the justifier of the one who has faith in Jesus.

ROMANS 3:24–26

But to him who does not work but believes on Him who justifies the ungodly, his faith is accounted for righteousness.

ROMANS 4:5

What shall we say then? That Gentiles, who did not pursue righteousness, have attained to righteous-ness, even the righteousness of faith.

ROMANS 9:30

For if by the one man's offense death reigned through the one, much more those who receive abundance of grace and of the gift of righteousness will reign in life through the One, Jesus Christ.

ROMANS 5:17

"In righteousness you shall be established;
  You shall be far from oppression, for you shall
      not fear;
  And from terror, for it shall not come near you.
  Indeed they shall surely assemble, but not
      because of Me.
  Whoever assembles against you shall fall for
      your sake. . . .
No weapon formed against you shall prosper,
  And every tongue which rises against you in
      judgment
  You shall condemn.
  This is the heritage of the servants of the LORD,
  And their righteousness is from Me,"
  Says the LORD.

ISAIAH 54:14–15, 17

For what the law could not do in that it was weak through the flesh, God did by sending His own Son in the likeness of sinful flesh, on account of sin: He condemned sin in the flesh, that the righteous requirement of the law might be fulfilled in us who do not walk according to the flesh but according to the Spirit.

ROMANS 8:3–4

For whom He foreknew, He also predestined to be conformed to the image of His Son, that He might be the firstborn among many brethren. Moreover whom He predestined, these He also called; whom He called, these He also justified; and whom He justified, these He also glorified.

ROMANS 8:29–30

The work of righteousness will be peace,
And the effect of righteousness, quietness and assurance forever.

ISAIAH 32:17

And if Christ is in you, the body is dead because of sin, but the Spirit is life because of righteousness.

ROMANS 8:10

For with the heart one believes unto righteousness, and with the mouth confession is made unto salvation.

ROMANS 10:10

Not by works of righteousness which we have done, but according to His mercy He saved us, through the washing of regeneration and renewing of the Holy Spirit.

TITUS 3:5

JESUS IS YOUR . . .

# DELIVERER

---

The Spirit of the Lord G<small>OD</small> is upon Me,
    Because the L<small>ORD</small> has anointed Me
    To preach good tidings to the poor;
    He has sent Me to heal the brokenhearted,
    To proclaim liberty to the captives,
    And the opening of the prison to those who are
        bound.

ISAIAH 61:1

And you shall know the truth, and the truth shall make you free. . . .
    Therefore if the Son makes you free, you shall be free indeed.

JOHN 8:32, 36

For the law of the Spirit of life in Christ Jesus has made me free from the law of sin and death.

ROMANS 8:2

Behold, I give you the authority to trample on serpents and scorpions, and over all the power of the
enemy, and nothing shall by any means hurt you.

LUKE 10:19

But now having been set free from sin, and having
become slaves of God, you have your fruit to holi-
ness, and the end, everlasting life.

ROMANS 6:22

The Spirit of the Lord is upon Me,
    Because he has anointed Me
    To preach the gospel to the poor;
    He has sent Me to heal the brokenhearted,
    To proclaim liberty to the captives
    And recovery of sight to the blind,
    To set at liberty those who are oppressed.

LUKE 4:18

For You have broken the yoke of his burden
    And the staff of his shoulder,
    The rod of his oppressor,
    As in the day of Midian.

ISAIAH 9:4

Now the Lord is the Spirit; and where the Spirit of the Lord is, there is liberty.

2 CORINTHIANS 3:17

Beloved, do not believe every spirit, but test the spirits, whether they are of God; because many false prophets have gone out into the world. By this you know the Spirit of God: Every spirit that confesses that Jesus Christ has come in the flesh is of God, and every spirit that does not confess that Jesus Christ has come in the flesh is not of God. And this is the spirit of the Antichrist, which you have heard was coming, and is now already in the world.

You are of God, little children, and have overcome them, because He who is in you is greater than he who is in the world.

1 JOHN 4:1–4

And these signs will follow those who believe: In My name they will cast out demons; they will speak with new tongues.

MARK 16:17

And they overcame him by the blood of the Lamb and by the word of their testimony, and they did not love their lives to the death.

REVELATION 12:11

JESUS IS YOUR . . .

# FELLOWSHIP

That which we have seen and heard we declare to you, that you also may have fellowship with us; and truly our fellowship is with the Father and with His Son Jesus Christ.

1 JOHN 1:3

Behold, I stand at the door and knock. If anyone hears My voice and opens the door, I will come in to him and dine with him, and he with Me.

REVELATION 3:20

Jesus answered and said to him, "If anyone loves Me, he will keep My word; and My Father will love him, and We will come to him and make Our home with him."

JOHN 14:23

God is faithful, by whom you were called into the fellowship of his Son, Jesus Christ our Lord.

1 CORINTHIANS 1:9

He who has My commandments and keeps them, it is he who loves Me. And he who loves Me will be loved by My Father, and I will love him and manifest Myself to him.

JOHN 14:21

Abide in Me, and I in you. As the branch cannot bear fruit of itself, unless it abides in the vine, neither can you, unless you abide in Me.

I am the vine, you are the branches. He who abides in me, and I in him, bears much fruit; for without Me you can do nothing. . . .

If you abide in Me, and My words abide in you, you will ask what you desire, and it shall be done for you.

JOHN 15:4–5, 7

Therefore if there is any consolation in Christ, if any comfort of love, if any fellowship of the Spirit, if any affection and mercy, fulfill my joy by being like-minded, having the same love, being of one accord, of one mind.

PHILIPPIANS 2:1–2

And walk in love, as Christ also has loved us and given Himself for us, an offering and a sacrifice to God for a sweet-smelling aroma. . . .

Speaking to one another in psalms and hymns and spiritual songs, singing and making melody in your heart to the Lord. . . .

For we are members of His body, of His flesh and of His bones.

EPHESIANS 5:2, 19, 30

I am a companion of all who fear You,
And of those who keep Your precepts.

PSALM 119:63

"Sing and rejoice, O daughter of Zion! For behold, I am coming and I will dwell in your midst," says the LORD.

ZECHARIAH 2:10

For where two or three are gathered together in My name, I am there in the midst of them.

MATTHEW 18:20

This is the message which we have heard from Him and declare to you, that God is light and in Him is no darkness at all. If we say that we have fellowship with Him, and walk in darkness, we lie and do not practice the truth. But if we walk in the light as He is in the light, we have fellowship with one another, and the blood of Jesus Christ His Son cleanses us from all sin.

1 JOHN 1:5–7

JESUS IS YOUR . . .

# EXAMPLE

For to this you were called, because Christ also suffered for us, leaving us an example, that you should follow His steps.

1 PETER 2:21

He who says he abides in Him ought himself also to walk just as He walked.

1 JOHN 2:6

Therefore be imitators of God as dear children. And walk in love, as Christ also has loved us and given himself for us, an offering and a sacrifice to God for a sweet-smelling aroma.

EPHESIANS 5:1–2

By this we know love, because He laid down His life for us. And we also ought to lay down our lives for the brethren.

1 JOHN 3:16

Let this mind be in you which was also in Christ Jesus, who, being in the form of God, did not consider it robbery to be equal with God, but made Himself of no reputation, taking the form of a bondservant, and coming in the likeness of men. And being found in appearance as a man, He humbled Himself and became obedient to the point of death, even the death of the cross.

PHILIPPIANS 2:5–8

Yet it shall not be so among you; but whoever desires to become great among you shall be your servant. And whoever of you desires to be first shall be slave of all. For even the Son of Man did not come to be served, but to serve, and to give His life a ransom for many.

MARK 10:43–45

A new commandment I give to you, that you love one another; as I have loved you, that you also love one another.

JOHN 13:34

If I then, your Lord and Teacher, have washed your feet, you also ought to wash one another's feet. For I have given you an example, that you should do as I have done to you.

JOHN 13:14–15

Now may the God of patience and comfort grant you to be like-minded toward one another, according to Christ Jesus, that you may with one mind and one mouth glorify the God and Father of our Lord Jesus Christ.

Therefore receive one another, just as Christ also received us, to the glory of God.

ROMANS 15:5–7

Bearing with one another, and forgiving one another, if anyone has a complaint against another; even as Christ forgave you, so you also must do.

COLOSSIANS 3:13

# COMPANION

A man who has friends must himself be friendly,
    But there is a friend who sticks closer than a
        brother.

PROVERBS 18:24

Let your conduct be without covetousness; be content with such things as you have. For He Himself has said, "I will never leave you nor forsake you."

HEBREWS 13:5

No longer do I call you servants, for a servant does not know what his master is doing; but I have called you friends, for all things that I heard from My Father I have made known to you. You did not choose Me, but I chose you and appointed you that you should go and bear fruit, and that your fruit should remain, that whatever you ask the Father in My name He may give you.

JOHN 15:15–16

This is My commandment, that you love one another as I have loved you. Greater love has no one than this, than to lay down one's life for his friends. You are My friends if you do whatever I command you.

JOHN 15:12–14

But if we walk in the light as He is in the light, we have fellowship with one another, and the blood of Jesus Christ His Son cleanses us from all sin.

1 JOHN 1:7

"For the mountains shall depart
    And the hills be removed,
    But My kindness shall not depart from you,
    Nor shall My covenant of peace be removed,"
    Says the Lord, who has mercy on you.

ISAIAH 54:10

Behold, I stand at the door and knock. If anyone hears My voice and opens the door, I will come in to him and dine with him, and he with Me.

REVELATION 3:20

I am a companion of all who fear You,
   And of those who keep Your precepts.

PSALM 119:63

Draw near to God and He will draw near to you. Cleanse your hands, you sinners; and purify your hearts, you double-minded.

JAMES 4:8

When my father and my mother forsake me,
   Then the LORD will take care of me.

PSALM 27:10

God is faithful, by whom you were called into the fellowship of His Son, Jesus Christ our Lord.

1 CORINTHIANS 1:9

That which we have seen and heard we declare to you, that you also may have fellowship with us; and truly our fellowship is with the Father and with his Son Jesus Christ.

1 JOHN 1:3

JESUS IS YOUR . . .

# BROTHER

---

For whoever does the will of my Father in heaven is My brother and sister and mother.

MATTHEW 12:50

For both He who sanctifies and those who are being sanctified are all of one, for which reason He is not ashamed to call them brethren.

HEBREWS 2:11

For whom He foreknew, He also predestined to be conformed to the image of His Son, that He might be the firstborn among many brethren.

ROMANS 8:29

But as many as received Him, to them He gave the right to become children of God, to those who believe in His name.

JOHN 1:12

For you are all sons of God through faith in Christ Jesus.

GALATIANS 3:26

Now, therefore, you are no longer strangers and foreigners, but fellow citizens with the saints and members of the household of God.

EPHESIANS 2:19

Behold what manner of love the Father has bestowed on us, that we should be called children of God! Therefore the world does not know us, because it did not know Him.

1 JOHN 3:1

And because you are sons, God has sent forth the Spirit of His Son into your hearts, crying out, "Abba, Father!" Therefore you are no longer a slave but a son, and if a son, then an heir of God through Christ.

GALATIANS 4:6–7

For as many as are led by the Spirit of God, these are sons of God.

ROMANS 8:14

Beloved, now we are children of God; and it has not yet been revealed what we shall be, but we know that when He is revealed, we shall be like Him, for we shall see Him as He is.

1 JOHN 3:2

JESUS IS YOUR . . .

# GUARDIAN

---

When you pass through the waters, I will be with
      you;
    And through the rivers, they shall not overflow
      you.
    When you walk through the fire, you shall not be
      burned,
    Nor shall the flame scorch you.

ISAIAH 43:2

For the eyes of the LORD run to and fro throughout
the whole earth, to show Himself strong on behalf of
those whose heart is loyal to Him. In this you have
done foolishly; therefore from now on you shall have
wars.

2 CHRONICLES 16:9

But You, O LORD, are a shield for me,
    My glory and the One who lifts up my head.

PSALM 3:3

The LORD your God, who goes before you, He will fight for you, according to all He did for you in Egypt before your eyes.

DEUTERONOMY 1:30

But the Lord is faithful, who will establish you and guard you from the evil one.

2 THESSALONIANS 3:3

But if you indeed obey His voice and do all that I speak, then I will be an enemy to your enemies and an adversary to your adversaries.

EXODUS 23:22

For You have been a shelter for me,
    A strong tower from the enemy.

PSALM 61:3

He will guard the feet of His saints,
    But the wicked shall be silent in darkness.
    "For by strength no man shall prevail."

1 SAMUEL 2:9

The LORD your God in your midst,
 The Mighty One, will save;
 He will rejoice over you with gladness,
 He will quiet you with His love,
 He will rejoice over you with singing.

         ZEPHANIAH 3:17


 For the eyes of the LORD are on the righteous,
 And His ears are open to their prayers;
 But the face of the LORD is against those who
  do evil.
And who is he who will harm you if you become fol-
lowers of what is good?

         1 PETER 3:12–13


The eternal God is your refuge,
 And underneath are the everlasting arms;
 He will thrust out the enemy from before you,
 And will say, "Destroy!"

        DEUTERONOMY 33:27

A thousand may fall at your side,
  And ten thousand at your right hand;
  But it shall not come near you.

PSALM 91:7

So shall they fear
  The name of the Lᴏʀᴅ from the west,
  And His glory from the rising of the sun;
  When the enemy comes in like a flood,
  The Spirit of the Lᴏʀᴅ will lift up a standard
    against him.

ISAIAH 59:19

JESUS IS YOUR . . .

# SECURITY

Blessed be the God and Father of our Lord Jesus Christ, who according to His abundant mercy has begotten us again to a living hope through the resurrection of Jesus Christ from the dead, to an inheritance incorruptible and undefiled and that does not fade away, reserved in heaven for you, who are kept by the power of God through faith for salvation ready to be revealed in the last time.

1 PETER 1:3–5

Being confident of this very thing, that He who has begun a good work in you will complete it until the day of Jesus Christ.

PHILIPPIANS 1:6

Surely goodness and mercy shall follow me
　　All the days of my life;
　　And I will dwell in the house of the Lord
　　Forever.

PSALM 23:6

My sheep hear My voice, and I know them, and they follow Me. And I give them eternal life, and they shall never perish; neither shall anyone snatch them out of My hand. My Father, who has given them to Me, is greater than all; and no one is able to snatch them out of My Father's hand.

JOHN 10:27–29

For I am persuaded that neither death nor life, nor angels nor principalities nor powers, nor things present nor things to come, nor height nor depth, nor any other created thing, shall be able to separate us from the love of God which is in Christ Jesus our Lord.

ROMANS 8:38–39

But the Lord is faithful, who will establish you and guard you from the evil one.

2 THESSALONIANS 3:3

Who also has sealed us and given us the Spirit in our hearts as a guarantee.

2 CORINTHIANS 1:22

Now to Him who is able to keep you from stumbling,
    And to present you faultless
    Before the presence of His glory with
         exceeding joy,
    To God our Savior,
    Who alone is wise,
    Be glory and majesty,
    Dominion and power,
    Both now and forever.
    Amen.

JUDE VV. 24–25

And do not grieve the Holy Spirit of God, by whom you were sealed for the day of redemption.

EPHESIANS 4:30

Lift up your eyes on high,
    And see who has created these things,
    Who brings out their host by number;
    He calls them all by name,
    By the greatness of His might
    And the strength of His power;
    Not one is missing.

ISAIAH 40:26

Do not labor for the food which perishes, but for the food which endures to everlasting life, which the Son of Man will give you, because God the Father has set his seal on Him.

JOHN 6:27

And we desire that each one of you show the same diligence to the full assurance of hope until the end, that you do not become sluggish, but imitate those who through faith and patience inherit the promises. . . .

That by two immutable things, in which it is impossible for God to lie, we might have strong consolation, who have fled for refuge to lay hold of the hope set before us.

This hope we have as an anchor of the soul, both sure and steadfast, and which enters the Presence behind the veil, where the forerunner has entered for us, even Jesus, having become High Priest forever according to the order of Melchizedek.

HEBREWS 6:11–12, 18–20

In Him you also trusted, after you heard the word of truth, the gospel of your salvation; in whom also, having believed, you were sealed with the Holy Spirit of promise.

EPHESIANS 1:13

All that the Father gives Me will come to Me, and the one who comes to Me I will by no means cast out.

JOHN 6:37

JESUS IS YOUR . . .

# SUFFICIENCY

And God is able to make all grace abound toward you, that you, always having all sufficiency in all things, may have an abundance for every good work.

2 CORINTHIANS 9:8

And my God shall supply all your need according to His riches in glory by Christ Jesus.

PHILIPPIANS 4:19

Therefore I say to you, whatever things you ask when you pray, believe that you receive them, and you will have them.

MARK 11:24

Not that we are sufficient of ourselves to think of anything as being from ourselves, but our sufficiency is from God.

2 CORINTHIANS 3:5

I can do all things through Christ who strengthens me.

PHILIPPIANS 4:13

And what is the exceeding greatness of His power toward us who believe, according to the working of His mighty power.

EPHESIANS 1:19

And He said to me, "My grace is sufficient for you, for My strength is made perfect in weakness." Therefore most gladly I will rather boast in my infirmities, that the power of Christ may rest upon me.

2 CORINTHIANS 12:9

Yet in all these things we are more than conquerors through Him who loved us.

ROMANS 8:37

Blessed be the God and Father of our Lord Jesus Christ, who has blessed us with every spiritual blessing in the heavenly places in Christ.

EPHESIANS 1:3

If you abide in Me, and My words abide in you, you will ask what you desire, and it shall be done for you.

JOHN 15:7

And in that day you will ask Me nothing. Most assuredly, I say to you, whatever you ask the Father in My name he will give you. Until now you have asked nothing in My name. Ask, and you will receive, that your joy may be full.

JOHN 16:23–24

And whatever things you ask in prayer, believing, you will receive.

MATTHEW 21:22

As His divine power has given to us all things that pertain to life and godliness, through the knowledge of Him who called us by glory and virtue, by which have been given to us exceedingly great and precious promises, that through these you may be partakers of the divine nature, having escaped the corruption that is in the world through lust.

2 PETER 1:3–4

He who did not spare His own Son, but delivered Him up for us all, how shall He not with Him also freely give us all things?

ROMANS 8:32

And whatever you ask in My name, that I will do, that the Father may be glorified in the Son.

JOHN 14:13

Bless the Lord, O my soul,
And forget not all His benefits:
Who forgives all your iniquities,
Who heals all your diseases,
Who redeems your life from destruction,
Who crowns you with lovingkindness and tender
mercies.

PSALM 103:2–4

JESUS IS YOUR . . .

# FULFILLMENT

Blessed are those who hunger and thirst for
            righteousness,
    For they shall be filled.

MATTHEW 5:6

You shall eat in plenty and be satisfied,
    And praise the name of the Lord your God,
    Who has dealt wondrously with you;
    And My people shall never be put to shame.

JOEL 2:26

Delight yourself also in the Lord,
    And He shall give you the desires of your heart.

PSALM 37:4

For He satisfies the longing soul,
    And fills the hungry soul with goodness.

PSALM 107:9

Who satisfies your mouth with good things,
So that your youth is renewed like the eagle's.

PSALM 103:5

And Jesus said to them, "I am the bread of life. He who comes to Me shall never hunger, and he who believes in Me shall never thirst."

JOHN 6:35

The poor shall eat and be satisfied;
Those who seek Him will praise the LORD.
Let your heart live forever!

PSALM 22:26

Jesus answered and said to her, "Whoever drinks of this water will thirst again, but whoever drinks of the water that I shall give him will never thirst. But the water that I shall give him will become in him a fountain of water springing up into everlasting life."

JOHN 4:13–14

If you extend your soul to the hungry
And satisfy the afflicted soul,
Then your light shall dawn in the darkness,

And your darkness shall be as the noonday.
The LORD will guide you continually,
And satisfy your soul in drought,
And strengthen your bones;
You shall be like a watered garden,
And like a spring of water, whose waters do
    not fail.

ISAIAH 58:10–11

The LORD will answer and say to His people,
    "Behold, I will send you grain and new wine
        and oil,
    And you will be satisfied by them;
    I will no longer make you a reproach among
        the nations."

JOEL 2:19

The eyes of all look expectantly to You,
    And You give them their food in due season.
    You open Your hand
    And satisfy the desire of every living thing.

PSALM 145:15–16

I will satiate the soul of the priests with abundance,
　　And My people shall be satisfied with My
　　　　goodness, says the LORD.

JEREMIAH 31:14

Why do you spend money for what is not bread,
　　And your wages for what does not satisfy?
　　Listen carefully to Me, and eat what is good,
　　And let your soul delight itself in abundance.

ISAIAH 55:2

My soul shall be satisfied as with marrow and
　　　　fatness?
　　And my mouth shall praise You with joyful lips.
　　When I remember You on my bed,
　　I meditate on You in the night watches.

PSALM 63:5–6

He who did not spare His own Son, but delivered
Him up for us all, how shall He not with Him also
freely give us all things?

ROMANS 8:32

JESUS IS YOUR . . .

# EVERYTHING

And my God shall supply all your need according to His riches in glory by Christ Jesus.

PHILIPPIANS 4:19

I can do all things through Christ who strengthens me.

PHILIPPIANS 4:13

Therefore let no one boast in men. For all things are yours: whether Paul or Apollos or Cephas, or the world or life or death, or things present or things to come—all are yours. And you are Christ's, and Christ is God's.

1 CORINTHIANS 3:21–23

Yet in all these things we are more than conquerors through Him who loved us.

ROMANS 8:37

Blessed be the Lord,

Who daily loads us with benefits?

The God of our salvation! Selah

PSALM 68:19

And in that day you will ask Me nothing. Most assuredly, I say to you, whatever you ask the Father in My name He will give you. Until now you have asked nothing in My name. Ask, and you will receive, that your joy may be full.

JOHN 16:23–24

Blessed be the God and Father of our Lord Jesus Christ, who has blessed us with every spiritual blessing in the heavenly places in Christ.

EPHESIANS 1:3

Now to Him who is able to do exceedingly abundantly above all that we ask or think, according to the power that works in us, to Him be glory in the church by Christ Jesus to all generations, forever and ever. Amen.

EPHESIANS 3:20–21

And whatever we ask we receive from Him, because we keep His commandments and do those things that are pleasing in His sight.

1 JOHN 3:22

If you abide in Me, and My words abide in you, you will ask what you desire, and it shall be done for you.

JOHN 15:7

Therefore I say to you, whatever things you ask when you pray, believe that you receive them, and you will have them.

MARK 11:24

Therefore, if anyone is in Christ, he is a new creation; old things have passed away; behold, all things have become new.

2 CORINTHIANS 5:17

And God is able to make all grace abound toward you, that you, always having all sufficiency in all things, may have an abundance for every good work.

2 CORINTHIANS 9:8

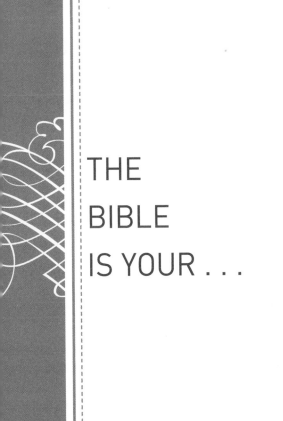

THE
BIBLE
IS YOUR . . .

THE BIBLE IS YOUR . . .

# INFALLIBLE AUTHORITY

All Scripture is given by inspiration of God, and is profitable for doctrine, for reproof, for correction, for instruction in righteousness.

2 TIMOTHY 3:16

Knowing this first, that no prophecy of Scripture is of any private interpretation, for prophecy never came by the will of man, but holy men of God spoke as they were moved by the Holy Spirit.

2 PETER 1:20–21

You search the Scriptures, for in them you think you have eternal life; and these are they which testify of Me.

JOHN 5:39

Having been born again, not of corruptible seed but incorruptible, through the word of God which lives and abides forever.

1 PETER 1:23

For the word of God is living and powerful, and sharper than any two-edged sword, piercing even to the division of soul and spirit, and of joints and marrow, and is a discerner of the thoughts and intents of the heart.

HEBREWS 4:12

For as the rain comes down, and the snow from
        heaven,
    And do not return there,
    But water the earth,
    And make it bring forth and bud,
    That it may give seed to the sower
    And bread to the eater,
    So shall My word be that goes forth from My
        mouth;
    It shall not return to Me void,
    But it shall accomplish what I please,
    And it shall prosper in the thing for which I sent it.

ISAIAH 55:10–11

For He spoke, and it was done;
    He commanded, and it stood fast.

PSALM 33:9

Every word of God is pure;
   He is a shield to those who put their trust in Him.

PROVERBS 30:5

Forever, O Lord,
   Your word is settled in heaven.

PSALM 119:89

By the word of the Lord the heavens were made,
   And all the host of them by the breath of His
      mouth.

PSALM 33:6

For all the promises of God in Him are Yes, and in
Him Amen, to the glory of God through us.

2 CORINTHIANS 1:20

Because
   "All flesh is as grass,
   And all the glory of man as the flower of the grass.
   The grass withers,
   And its flower falls away,
   But the word of the Lord endures forever."

1 PETER 1:24–25

THE BIBLE IS YOUR . . .

# DEED OF INHERITANCE

So now, brethren, I commend you to God and to the word of His grace, which is able to build you up and give you an inheritance among all those who are sanctified.

ACTS 20:32

To open their eyes, in order to turn them from darkness to light, and from the power of Satan to God, that they may receive forgiveness of sins and an inheritance among those who are sanctified by faith in Me.

ACTS 26:18

The Spirit Himself bears witness with our spirit that we are children of God, and if children, then heirs—heirs of God and joint heirs with Christ, if indeed we suffer with Him, that we may also be glorified together.

ROMANS 8:16–17

In Him also we have obtained an inheritance, being predestined according to the purpose of Him who works all things according to the counsel of His will, that we who first trusted in Christ should be to the praise of His glory.

In Him you also trusted, after you heard the word of truth, the gospel of your salvation; in whom also, having believed, you were sealed with the Holy Spirit of promise, who is the guarantee of our inheritance until the redemption of the purchased possession, to the praise of His glory.

EPHESIANS 1:11–14

And if you are Christ's, then you are Abraham's seed, and heirs according to the promise.

GALATIANS 3:29

That the Gentiles should be fellow heirs, of the same body, and partakers of His promise in Christ through the gospel.

EPHESIANS 3:6

For all the promises of God in Him are Yes, and in Him Amen, to the glory of God through us.

2 CORINTHIANS 1:20

But now they desire a better, that is, a heavenly country. Therefore God is not ashamed to be called their God, for He has prepared a city for them.

HEBREWS 11:16

Then the King will say to those on His right hand, "Come, you blessed of My Father, inherit the kingdom prepared for you from the foundation of the world."

MATTHEW 25:34

In my Father's house are many mansions; if it were not so, I would have told you. I go to prepare a place for you. And if I go and prepare a place for you, I will come again and receive you to Myself; that where I am, there you may be also.

JOHN 14:2–3

But as it is written:

"Eye has not seen, nor ear heard,
Nor have entered into the heart of man
The things which God has prepared for those
who love Him."

1 CORINTHIANS 2:9

By which have been given to us exceedingly great and precious promises, that through these you may be partakers of the divine nature, having escaped the corruption that is in the world through lust.

2 PETER 1:4

And whatever you do, do it heartily, as to the Lord and not to men, knowing that from the Lord you will receive the reward of the inheritance; for you serve the Lord Christ.

COLOSSIANS 3:23–24

Wait on the LORD,
And keep His way,
And He shall exalt you to inherit the land;
When the wicked are cut off, you shall see it.

PSALM 37:34

THE BIBLE IS YOUR . . .

# GUIDE FOR LIFE

Your word is a lamp to my feet
    And a light to my path.

PSALM 119:105

When you roam, they will lead you;
    When you sleep, they will keep you;
    And when you awake, they will speak with you.
    For the commandment is a lamp,
    And the law a light;
    Reproofs of instruction are the way of life.

PROVERBS 6:22–23

Your word I have hidden in my heart,
    That I might not sin against You.

PSALM 119:11

Moreover by them Your servant is warned,
    And in keeping them there is great reward.

PSALM 19:11

By which have been given to us exceedingly great and precious promises, that through these you may be partakers of the divine nature, having escaped the corruption that is in the world through lust.

2 PETER 1:4

How can a young man cleanse his way?
By taking heed according to Your word.

PSALM 119:9

Then Jesus said to those Jews who believed Him, "If you abide in My word, you are My disciples indeed. And you shall know the truth, and the truth shall make you free."

JOHN 8:31–32

Your testimonies also are my delight
And my counselors.

PSALM 119:24

The steps of a good man are ordered by the LORD,
And He delights in his way.

PSALM 37:23

I will instruct you and teach you in the way you
       should go;
  I will guide you with My eye.

PSALM 32:8

He restores my soul;
  He leads me in the paths of righteousness
  For His name's sake.

PSALM 23:3

Your ears shall hear a word behind you, saying,
  "This is the way, walk in it,"
  Whenever you turn to the right hand
  Or whenever you turn to the left.

ISAIAH 30:21

This Book of the Law shall not depart from your
mouth, but you shall meditate in it day and night, that
you may observe to do according to all that is written
in it. For then you will make your way prosperous,
and then you will have good success.

JOSHUA 1:8

All Scripture is given by inspiration of God, and is profitable for doctrine, for reproof, for correction, for instruction in righteousness, that the man of God may be complete, thoroughly equipped for every good work.

2 TIMOTHY 3:16–17

As He spoke by the mouth of His holy prophets,
Who have been since the world began . . .
To give light to those who sit in darkness and the
shadow of death,
To guide our feet into the way of peace.

LUKE 1:70, 79

THE BIBLE IS YOUR . . .

# STABILITY

---

Having been born again, not of corruptible seed but incorruptible, through the word of God which lives and abides forever, because

"All flesh is as grass,

And all the glory of man as the flower of the
grass.

The grass withers,

And its flower falls away,

But the word of the LORD endures forever."

Now this is the word which by the gospel was preached to you.

1 PETER 1:23–25

"For I am the LORD. I speak, and the word which I speak will come to pass; it will no more be postponed; for in your days, O rebellious house, I will say the word and perform it," says the Lord GOD.

EZEKIEL 12:25

My son, give attention to my words;
  Incline your ear to my sayings.
  Do not let them depart from your eyes;
  Keep them in the midst of your heart;
  For they are life to those who find them,
  And health to all their flesh.

PROVERBS 4:20–22

The grass withers, the flower fades,
  But the word of our God stands forever.

ISAIAH 40:8

Heaven and earth will pass away, but My words will by no means pass away.

MATTHEW 24:35

For assuredly, I say to you, till heaven and earth pass away, one jot or one tittle will by no means pass from the law till all is fulfilled.

MATTHEW 5:18

Forever, O Lord,
  Your word is settled in heaven.

PSALM 119:89

Blessed be the LORD, who has given rest to His people Israel, according to all that He promised. There has not failed one word of all His good promise, which He promised through His servant Moses.

1 KINGS 8:56

What then shall we say to these things? If God is for us, who can be against us?

ROMANS 8:31

Now to Him who is able to keep you from stumbling,
    And to present you faultless
    Before the presence of His glory with exceeding
         joy,
    To God our Savior,
    Who alone is wise,
    Be glory and majesty,
    Dominion and power,
    Both now and forever.
    Amen.

JUDE VV. 24–25

The eternal God is your refuge,
     And underneath are the everlasting arms;
     He will thrust out the enemy from before you,
     And will say, "Destroy!"

DEUTERONOMY 33:27

The name of the Lord is a strong tower;
     The righteous run to it and are safe.

PROVERBS 18:10

He also brought me up out of a horrible pit,
     Out of the miry clay,
     And set my feet upon a rock,
     And established my steps.

PSALM 40:2

God is our refuge and strength,
     A very present help in trouble.

PSALM 46:1

But the Lord is faithful, who will establish you and guard you from the evil one.

2 THESSALONIANS 3:3

THE BIBLE IS YOUR . . .

# STRENGTH

And he said, "O man greatly beloved, fear not! Peace be to you; be strong, yes, be strong!"

So when he spoke to me I was strengthened, and said, "Let my lord speak, for you have strengthened me."

DANIEL 10:19

For thus says the Lord God, the Holy One of Israel:
"In returning and rest you shall be saved;
In quietness and confidence shall be your
strength."
But you would not.

ISAIAH 30:15

That He would grant you, according to the riches of His glory, to be strengthened with might through His Spirit in the inner man, that Christ may dwell in your hearts through faith; that you, being rooted and grounded in love.

EPHESIANS 3:16–17

That you may walk worthy of the Lord, fully pleasing Him, being fruitful in every good work and increasing in the knowledge of God; strengthened with all might, according to His glorious power, for all patience and longsuffering with joy; giving thanks to the Father who has qualified us to be partakers of the inheritance of the saints in the light.

COLOSSIANS 1:10–12

But those who wait on the LORD
Shall renew their strength;
They shall mount up with wings like eagles,
They shall run and not be weary,
They shall walk and not faint.

ISAIAH 40:31

My soul melts from heaviness;
Strengthen me according to Your word.

PSALM 119:28

He gives power to the weak,
And to those who have no might He increases strength.

ISAIAH 40:29

Then he said to them, "Go your way, eat the fat, drink the sweet, and send portions to those for whom nothing is prepared; for this day is holy to our Lord. Do not sorrow, for the joy of the LORD is your strength."

NEHEMIAH 8:10

Fear not, for I am with you;
Be not dismayed, for I am your God.
I will strengthen you,
Yes, I will help you,
I will uphold you with My righteous right hand.

ISAIAH 41:10

I can do all things through Christ who strengthens me.

PHILIPPIANS 4:13

Counsel is mine, and sound wisdom;
I am understanding, I have strength.

PROVERBS 8:14

Finally, my brethren, be strong in the Lord and in the power of His might.

EPHESIANS 6:10

The LORD is my rock and my fortress and my
deliverer;
My God, my strength, in whom I will trust;
My shield and the horn of my salvation, my
stronghold.

PSALM 18:2

Therefore take up the whole armor of God, that you
may be able to withstand in the evil day, and having
done all, to stand.

EPHESIANS 6:13

The LORD is my light and my salvation;
Whom shall I fear?
The LORD is the strength of my life;
Of whom shall I be afraid?

PSALM 27:1

# WHAT TO
# DO WHEN
# YOU FEEL . . .

WHAT TO DO WHEN YOU FEEL . . .

# DISCOURAGED

So the ransomed of the LORD shall return
  And come to Zion with singing,
  With everlasting joy on their heads.
  They shall obtain joy and gladness;
  Sorrow and sighing shall flee away.

ISAIAH 51:11

Though I walk in the midst of trouble, You will
        revive me;
  You will stretch out Your hand
  Against the wrath of my enemies,
  And Your right hand will save me.

PSALM 138:7

Peace I leave with you, My peace I give to you; not
as the world gives do I give to you. Let not your heart
be troubled, neither let it be afraid.

JOHN 14:27

In this you greatly rejoice, though now for a little while, if need be, you have been grieved by various trials, that the genuineness of your faith, being much more precious than gold that perishes, though it is tested by fire, may be found to praise, honor, and glory at the revelation of Jesus Christ, whom having not seen you love. Though now you do not see Him, yet believing, you rejoice with joy inexpressible and full of glory, receiving the end of your faith—the salvation of your souls.

1 PETER 1:6–9

We are hard-pressed on every side, yet not crushed; we are perplexed, but not in despair; persecuted, but not forsaken; struck down, but not destroyed.

2 CORINTHIANS 4:8–9

Therefore do not cast away your confidence, which has great reward. For you have need of endurance, so that after you have done the will of God, you may receive the promise.

HEBREWS 10:35–36

Be anxious for nothing, but in everything by prayer and supplication, with thanksgiving, let your requests be made known to God; and the peace of God, which surpasses all understanding, will guard your hearts and minds through Christ Jesus.

Finally, brethren, whatever things are true, whatever things are noble, whatever things are just, whatever things are pure, whatever things are lovely, whatever things are of good report, if there is any virtue and if there is anything praiseworthy—meditate on these things.

PHILIPPIANS 4:6–8

Let not your heart be troubled; you believe in God, believe also in Me.

JOHN 14:1

Being confident of this very thing, that He who has begun a good work in you will complete it until the day of Jesus Christ.

PHILIPPIANS 1:6

The LORD is my light and my salvation;
   Whom shall I fear?
   The LORD is the strength of my life;
   Of whom shall I be afraid?
   When the wicked came against me
   To eat up my flesh,
   My enemies and foes,
   They stumbled and fell.
   Though an army may encamp against me,
   My heart shall not fear;
   Though war may rise against me,
   In this I will be confident. . . .
And now my head shall be lifted up above my
         enemies all around me;
   Therefore I will offer sacrifices of joy in His
      tabernacle;
   I will sing, yes, I will sing praises to the LORD.

PSALM 27:1–3, 6

And let us not grow weary while doing good, for in
due season we shall reap if we do not lose heart.

GALATIANS 6:9

Be of good courage,
    And He shall strengthen your heart,
    All you who hope in the Lord.

PSALM 31:24

WHAT TO DO WHEN YOU FEEL . . .

# WORRIED

Casting all your care upon Him, for He cares for you.

1 PETER 5:7

Let not your heart be troubled; you believe in God, believe also in Me.

JOHN 14:1

And let the peace of God rule in your hearts, to which also you were called in one body; and be thankful.

COLOSSIANS 3:15

You will keep him in perfect peace,
    Whose mind is stayed on You,
    Because he trusts in You.

ISAIAH 26:3

When you lie down, you will not be afraid;
    Yes, you will lie down and your sleep will be
        sweet.

PROVERBS 3:24

Be anxious for nothing, but in everything by prayer and supplication, with thanksgiving, let your requests be made known to God; and the peace of God, which surpasses all understanding, will guard your hearts and minds through Christ Jesus.

PHILIPPIANS 4:6–7

I will both lie down in peace, and sleep;
For you alone, O LORD, make me dwell in safety.

PSALM 4:8

For we who have believed do enter that rest, as He has said:
"So I swore in my wrath,
'They shall not enter my rest,'"
although the works were finished from the foundation of the world. . . .
There remains therefore a rest for the people of God.

HEBREWS 4:3, 9

And my God shall supply all your need according to His riches in glory by Christ Jesus.

PHILIPPIANS 4:19

For to be carnally minded is death, but to be spiritually minded is life and peace.

ROMANS 8:6

Great peace have those who love Your law,
And nothing causes them to stumble.

PSALM 119:165

He who dwells in the secret place of the Most High
Shall abide under the shadow of the Almighty.
I will say of the LORD, "He is my refuge and my
fortress;
My God, in Him I will trust."

PSALM 91:1–2

Peace I leave with you, my peace I give to you; not as the world gives do I give to you. Let not your heart be troubled, neither let it be afraid.

JOHN 14:27

Therefore I say to you, do not worry about your life, what you will eat or what you will drink; nor about your body, what you will put on. Is not life more than food and the body more than clothing? Look at the birds of the air, for they neither sow nor reap nor gather into barns; yet your heavenly Father feeds them. Are you not of more value than they? Which of you by worrying can add one cubit to his stature? . . .

Therefore do not worry, saying, "What shall we eat?" or "What shall we drink?" or "What shall we wear?" For after all these things the Gentiles seek. For your heavenly Father knows that you need all these things. But seek first the kingdom of God and His righteousness, and all these things shall be added to you. Therefore do not worry about tomorrow, for tomorrow will worry about its own things. Sufficient for the day is its own trouble.

MATTHEW 6:25–27, 31–34

WHAT TO DO WHEN YOU FEEL . . .

# LONELY

Let your conduct be without covetousness; be content with such things as you have. For He Himself has said, "I will never leave you nor forsake you."

HEBREWS 13:5

Teaching them to observe all things that I have commanded you; and lo, I am with you always, even to the end of the age. Amen.

MATTHEW 28:20

For the LORD will not forsake His people, for His great name's sake, because it has pleased the LORD to make you His people.

1 SAMUEL 12:22

The eternal God is your refuge,
    And underneath are the everlasting arms;
    He will thrust out the enemy from before you,
    And will say, "Destroy!"

DEUTERONOMY 33:27

Fear not, for I am with you;

Be not dismayed, for I am your God.

I will strengthen you,

Yes, I will help you,

I will uphold you with My righteous right hand.

ISAIAH 41:10

Who shall separate us from the love of Christ? Shall tribulation, or distress, or persecution, or famine, or nakedness, or peril, or sword?

As it is written:

"For Your sake we are killed all day long;

We are accounted as sheep for the slaughter."

Yet in all these things we are more than conquerors through Him who loved us. For I am persuaded that neither death nor life, nor angels nor principalities nor powers, nor things present nor things to come, nor height nor depth, nor any other created thing, shall be able to separate us from the love of God which is in Christ Jesus our Lord.

ROMANS 8:35–39

I will not leave you orphans; I will come to you.

JOHN 14:18

He heals the brokenhearted
And binds up their wounds.

PSALM 147:3

Let not your heart be troubled; you believe in God, believe also in Me.

JOHN 14:1

(For the LORD your God is a merciful God), He will not forsake you nor destroy you, nor forget the covenant of your fathers which He swore to them.

DEUTERONOMY 4:31

Be strong and of good courage, do not fear nor be afraid of them; for the LORD your God, He is the One who goes with you. He will not leave you nor forsake you.

DEUTERONOMY 31:6

When my father and my mother forsake me,
Then the LORD will take care of me.

PSALM 27:10

Casting all your care upon Him, for He cares for you.

1 PETER 5:7

"For the mountains shall depart
   And the hills be removed,
   But My kindness shall not depart from you,
   Nor shall My covenant of peace be removed,"
   Says the Lord, who has mercy on you.

ISAIAH 54:10

God is our refuge and strength,
   A very present help in trouble.

PSALM 46:1

# DEPRESSED

The righteous cry out, and the LORD hears,
And delivers them out of all their troubles.

PSALM 34:17

To console those who mourn in Zion,
To give them beauty for ashes,
The oil of joy for mourning,
The garment of praise for the spirit of heaviness;
That they may be called trees of righteousness,
The planting of the LORD, that He may be
glorified.

ISAIAH 61:3

When you pass through the waters, I will be with you;
And through the rivers, they shall not overflow you.
When you walk through the fire, you shall not
be burned,
Nor shall the flame scorch you.

ISAIAH 43:2

Beloved, do not think it strange concerning the fiery trial which is to try you, as though some strange thing happened to you; but rejoice to the extent that you partake of Christ's sufferings, that when his glory is revealed, you may also be glad with exceeding joy.

1 PETER 4:12–13

He heals the brokenhearted
    And binds up their wounds.

PSALM 147:3

But those who wait on the LORD
    Shall renew their strength;
    They shall mount up with wings like eagles,
    They shall run and not be weary,
    They shall walk and not faint.

ISAIAH 40:31

For His anger is but for a moment,
    His favor is for life;
    Weeping may endure for a night,
    But joy comes in the morning.

PSALM 30:5

Blessed be the God and Father of our Lord Jesus Christ, the Father of mercies and God of all comfort, who comforts us in all our tribulation, that we may be able to comfort those who are in any trouble, with the comfort with which we ourselves are comforted by God.

2 CORINTHIANS 1:3–4

For I am persuaded that neither death nor life, nor angels nor principalities nor powers, nor things present nor things to come, nor height nor depth, nor any other created thing, shall be able to separate us from the love of God which is in Christ Jesus our Lord.

ROMANS 8:38–39

Fear not, for I am with you;
    Be not dismayed, for I am your God.
    I will strengthen you,
    Yes, I will help you,
    I will uphold you with My righteous right hand.

ISAIAH 41:10

Therefore humble yourselves under the mighty hand of God, that He may exalt you in due time, casting all your care upon Him, for He cares for you.

1 PETER 5:6–7

Then He spoke a parable to them, that men always ought to pray and not lose heart.

LUKE 18:1

Then he said to them, "Go your way, eat the fat, drink the sweet, and send portions to those for whom nothing is prepared; for this day is holy to our Lord. Do not sorrow, for the joy of the Lord is your strength."

NEHEMIAH 8:10

So the ransomed of the Lord shall return,
    And come to Zion with singing,
    With everlasting joy on their heads.
    They shall obtain joy and gladness;
    Sorrow and sighing shall flee away.

ISAIAH 51:11

WHAT TO DO WHEN YOU FEEL . . .

# DISSATISFIED

The young lions lack and suffer hunger;
　　But those who seek the LORD shall not lack any
　　　　good thing.

PSALM 34:10

For I will pour water on him who is thirsty,
　　And floods on the dry ground;
　　I will pour My Spirit on your descendants,
　　And My blessing on your offspring.

ISAIAH 44:3

Trust in the LORD, and do good;
　　Dwell in the land, and feed on His faithfulness.

PSALM 37:3

You shall eat in plenty and be satisfied,
　　And praise the name of the LORD your God,
　　Who has dealt wondrously with you;
　　And My people shall never be put to shame.

JOEL 2:26

O God, You are my God;
Early will I seek you;
My soul thirsts for You;
My flesh longs for You
In a dry and thirsty land
Where there is no water.
So I have looked for You in the sanctuary,
To see Your power and Your glory.
Because Your lovingkindness is better than life,
My lips shall praise You.
Thus I will bless You while I live;
I will lift up my hands in Your name.
My soul shall be satisfied as with marrow and
fatness,
And my mouth shall praise You with joyful lips.

PSALM 63:1–5

A man will be satisfied with good by the fruit of his
mouth,
And the recompense of a man's hands will be
rendered to him.

PROVERBS 12:14

I know how to be abased, and I know how to abound. Everywhere and in all things I have learned both to be full and to be hungry, both to abound and to suffer need. I can do all things through Christ who strengthens me.

PHILIPPIANS 4:12–13

Bless the LORD, O my soul;
    And all that is within me, bless his holy name!
    Bless the LORD, O my soul,
    And forget not all His benefits:
    Who forgives all your iniquities,
    Who heals all your diseases,
    Who redeems your life from destruction,
    Who crowns you with lovingkindness and tender
        mercies,
    Who satisfies your mouth with good things,
    So that your youth is renewed like the eagle's.

PSALM 103:1–5

For He satisfies the longing soul,
    And fills the hungry soul with goodness.

PSALM 107:9

Behold, God is my salvation,
    I will trust and not be afraid;
    For Y<small>AH</small>, the L<small>ORD</small>, is my strength and song;
    He also has become my salvation.
Therefore with joy you will draw water
    From the wells of salvation.

ISAIAH 12:2–3

And God is able to make all grace abound toward you, that you, always having all sufficiency in all things, may have an abundance for every good work.

2 CORINTHIANS 9:8

Ho! Everyone who thirsts,
    Come to the waters;
    And you who have no money,
    Come, buy and eat.
    Yes, come, buy wine and milk
    Without money and without price.

ISAIAH 55:1

And My people shall be satisfied with My goodness, says the L<small>ORD</small>.

JEREMIAH 31:14

WHAT TO DO WHEN YOU FEEL . . .

# CONDEMNED

There is therefore now no condemnation to those who are in Christ Jesus, who do not walk according to the flesh, but according to the Spirit.

ROMANS 8:1

He has not dealt with us according to our sins,
Nor punished us according to our iniquities. . . .
As far as the east is from the west,
So far has He removed our transgressions
from us.

PSALM 103:10, 12

Therefore, if anyone is in Christ, he is a new creation; old things have passed away; behold, all things have become new.

2 CORINTHIANS 5:17

Blessed is he whose transgression is forgiven,
Whose sin is covered.

PSALM 32:1

For God did not send His Son into the world to condemn the world, but that the world through Him might be saved.

He who believes in Him is not condemned; but he who does not believe is condemned already, because he has not believed in the name of the only begotten Son of God.

JOHN 3:17–18

Most assuredly, I say to you, he who hears My word and believes in Him who sent Me has everlasting life, and shall not come into judgment, but has passed from death into life.

JOHN 5:24

For I will be merciful to their unrighteousness, and their sins and their lawless deeds I will remember no more.

HEBREWS 8:12

If we confess our sins, He is faithful and just to forgive us our sins and to cleanse us from all unrighteousness.

1 JOHN 1:9

Let the wicked forsake his way,
And the unrighteous man his thoughts;
Let him return to the LORD,
And He will have mercy on him;
And to our God,
For He will abundantly pardon.

ISAIAH 55:7

I acknowledged my sin to You,
And my iniquity I have not hidden.
I said, "I will confess my transgressions to the
LORD,"
And You forgave the iniquity of my sin. Selah

PSALM 32:5

Then I heard a loud voice saying in heaven, "Now salvation, and strength, and the kingdom of our God, and the power of His Christ have come, for the accuser of our brethren, who accused them before our God day and night, has been cast down. And they overcame him by the blood of the Lamb and by the word of their testimony, and they did not love their lives to the death."

REVELATION 12:10–11

I, even I, am He who blots out your transgressions
        for My own sake;
    And I will not remember your sins.

ISAIAH 43:25

When Jesus had raised Himself up and saw no one but
the woman, He said to her, "Woman, where are those
accusers of yours? Has no one condemned you?"

    She said, "No one, Lord."

    And Jesus said to her, "Neither do I condemn you;
go and sin no more."

JOHN 8:10–11

"No more shall every man teach his neighbor, and
every man his brother, saying, 'Know the LORD,' for
they all shall know Me, from the least of them to the
greatest of them, says the LORD. For I will forgive
their iniquity, and their sin I will remember no more."

JEREMIAH 31:34

Let us draw near with a true heart in full assurance
of faith, having our hearts sprinkled from an evil conscience and our bodies washed with pure water.

HEBREWS 10:22

For if you return to the Lᴏʀᴅ, your brethren and your children will be treated with compassion by those who lead them captive, so that they may come back to this land; for the Lᴏʀᴅ your God is gracious and merciful, and will not turn His face from you if you return to Him.

2 CHRONICLES 30:9

# CONFUSED

For God is not the author of confusion but of peace, as in all the churches of the saints.

1 CORINTHIANS 14:33

For God has not given us a spirit of fear, but of power and of love and of a sound mind.

2 TIMOTHY 1:7

For where envy and self-seeking exist, confusion and every evil thing are there. But the wisdom that is from above is first pure, then peaceable, gentle, willing to yield, full of mercy and good fruits, without partiality and without hypocrisy. Now the fruit of righteousness is sown in peace by those who make peace.

JAMES 3:16–18

If any of you lacks wisdom, let him ask of God, who gives to all liberally and without reproach, and it will be given to him.

JAMES 1:5

For the Lord GOD will help Me;
Therefore I will not be disgraced;
Therefore I have set My face like a flint,
And I know that I will not be ashamed.

ISAIAH 50:7

Beloved, do not think it strange concerning the fiery trial which is to try you, as though some strange thing happened to you; but rejoice to the extent that you partake of Christ's sufferings, that when His glory is revealed, you may also be glad with exceeding joy.

1 PETER 4:12–13

Trust in the LORD with all your heart,
And lean not on your own understanding;
In all your ways acknowledge Him,
And He shall direct your paths.

PROVERBS 3:5–6

I will instruct you and teach you in the way you
should go;
I will guide you with My eye.

PSALM 32:8

Great peace have those who love Your law,
And nothing causes them to stumble.

PSALM 119:165

Cast your burden on the LORD,
And He shall sustain you;
He shall never permit the righteous to be moved.

PSALM 55:22

When you pass through the waters, I will be
with you;
And through the rivers, they shall not
overflow you.
When you walk through the fire, you shall not
be burned,
Nor shall the flame scorch you.

ISAIAH 43:2

He gives power to the weak,
And to those who have no might He increases
strength.

ISAIAH 40:29

Your ears shall hear a word behind you, saying,
"This is the way, walk in it,"
Whenever you turn to the right hand
Or whenever you turn to the left.

ISAIAH 30:21

Be anxious for nothing, but in everything by prayer and supplication, with thanksgiving, let your requests be made known to God; and the peace of God, which surpasses all understanding, will guard your hearts and minds through Christ Jesus.

PHILIPPIANS 4:6–7

# TEMPTED

Therefore let him who thinks he stands take heed lest he fall. No temptation has overtaken you except such as is common to man; but God is faithful, who will not allow you to be tempted beyond what you are able, but with the temptation will also make the way of escape, that you may be able to bear it.

1 CORINTHIANS 10:12–13

Seeing then that we have a great High Priest who has passed through the heavens, Jesus the Son of God, let us hold fast our confession. For we do not have a High Priest who cannot sympathize with our weaknesses, but was in all points tempted as we are, yet without sin. Let us therefore come boldly to the throne of grace, that we may obtain mercy and find grace to help in time of need.

HEBREWS 4:14–16

For in that He Himself has suffered, being tempted, He is able to aid those who are tempted.

HEBREWS 2:18

Then the Lord knows how to deliver the godly out of temptations.

2 PETER 2:9

For sin shall not have dominion over you, for you are not under law but under grace.

ROMANS 6:14

Your word I have hidden in my heart,
    That I might not sin against You.

PSALM 119:11

Let no one say when he is tempted, "I am tempted by God"; for God cannot be tempted by evil, nor does He Himself tempt anyone. But each one is tempted when he is drawn away by his own desires and enticed.

JAMES 1:13–14

He who covers his sins will not prosper,
But whoever confesses and forsakes them will
have mercy.

PROVERBS 28:13

Be sober, be vigilant; because your adversary the devil walks about like a roaring lion, seeking whom he may devour. Resist him, steadfast in the faith, knowing that the same sufferings are experienced by your brotherhood in the world.

1 PETER 5:8–9

Finally, my brethren, be strong in the Lord and in the power of His might. Put on the whole armor of God, that you may be able to stand against the wiles of the devil. . . .

Above all, taking the shield of faith with which you will be able to quench all the fiery darts of the wicked one.

EPHESIANS 6:10–11, 16

Therefore submit to God. Resist the devil and he will flee from you.

JAMES 4:7

You are of God, little children, and have overcome them, because He who is in you is greater than he who is in the world.

1 JOHN 4:4

My brethren, count it all joy when you fall into various trials, knowing that the testing of your faith produces patience. . . .

Blessed is the man who endures temptation; for when he has been approved, he will receive the crown of life which the Lord has promised to those who love Him.

JAMES 1:2–3, 12

Now to Him who is able to keep you from stumbling,
    And to present you faultless
    Before the presence of His glory with exceeding
        joy,
    To God our Savior,
    Who alone is wise,
    Be glory and majesty.

JUDE VV. 24–25

If we confess our sins, He is faithful and just to forgive us our sins and to cleanse us from all unrighteousness.

1 JOHN 1:9

In this you greatly rejoice, though now for a little while, if need be, you have been grieved by various trials, that the genuineness of your faith, being much more precious than gold that perishes, though it is tested by fire, may be found to praise, honor, and glory at the revelation of Jesus Christ.

1 PETER 1:6–7

WHAT TO DO WHEN YOU FEEL

# ANGRY

So then, my beloved brethren, let every man be swift to hear, slow to speak, slow to wrath; for the wrath of man does not produce the righteousness of God.

JAMES 1:19–20

"Be angry, and do not sin": do not let the sun go down on your wrath.

EPHESIANS 4:26

A soft answer turns away wrath,
But a harsh word stirs up anger.

PROVERBS 15:1

For if you forgive men their trespasses, your heavenly Father will also forgive you.

MATTHEW 6:14

He who is slow to wrath has great understanding,
But he who is impulsive exalts folly.

PROVERBS 14:29

Cease from anger, and forsake wrath;
Do not fret—it only causes harm.

PSALM 37:8

He who is slow to anger is better than the mighty,
And he who rules his spirit than he who takes
a city.

PROVERBS 16:32

Beloved, do not avenge yourselves, but rather give place to wrath; for it is written, "Vengeance is Mine, I will repay," says the Lord.

ROMANS 12:19

If your enemy is hungry, give him bread to eat;
And if he is thirsty, give him water to drink;
For so you will heap coals of fire on his head,
And the LORD will reward you.

PROVERBS 25:21–22

For we know Him who said, "Vengeance is Mine, I will repay," says the Lord. And again, "The LORD will judge His people."

HEBREWS 10:30

Let all bitterness, wrath, anger, clamor, and evil speaking be put away from you, with all malice. And be kind to one another, tenderhearted, forgiving one another, even as God in Christ forgave you.

EPHESIANS 4:31–32

But I say to you that whoever is angry with his brother without a cause shall be in danger of the judgment. And whoever says to his brother, "Raca!" shall be in danger of the council. But whoever says, "You fool!" shall be in danger of hell fire. Therefore if you bring your gift to the altar, and there remember that your brother has something against you, leave your gift there before the altar, and go your way. First be reconciled to your brother, and then come and offer your gift.

MATTHEW 5:22–24

A wise man fears and departs from evil,
    But a fool rages and is self-confident.
    A quick-tempered man acts foolishly,
    And a man of wicked intentions is hated.

PROVERBS 14:16–17

Do not hasten in your spirit to be angry,
  For anger rests in the bosom of fools.

ECCLESIASTES 7:9

But now you yourselves are to put off all these: anger, wrath, malice, blasphemy, filthy language out of your mouth.

COLOSSIANS 3:8

# REBELLIOUS

Obey those who rule over you, and be submissive, for they watch out for your souls, as those who must give account. Let them do so with joy and not with grief, for that would be unprofitable for you.

HEBREWS 13:17

A wise man fears and departs from evil,
But a fool rages and is self-confident.
A quick-tempered man acts foolishly,
And a man of wicked intentions is hated.

PROVERBS 14:16–17

Though He was a Son, yet He learned obedience by the things which He suffered.

HEBREWS 5:8

No grave trouble will overtake the righteous,
But the wicked shall be filled with evil.

PROVERBS 12:21

So Samuel said:

"Has the LORD as great delight in burnt offerings
and sacrifices,
As in obeying the voice of the LORD?
Behold, to obey is better than sacrifice,
And to heed than the fat of rams.
For rebellion is as the sin of witchcraft,
And stubbornness is as iniquity and idolatry.
Because you have rejected the word of the LORD,
He also has rejected you from being king."

1 SAMUEL 15:22–23

Therefore gird up the loins of your mind, be sober, and rest your hope fully upon the grace that is to be brought to you at the revelation of Jesus Christ; as obedient children, not conforming yourselves to the former lusts, as in your ignorance.

1 PETER 1:13–14

For you were once darkness, but now you are light in the Lord. Walk as children of light.

EPHESIANS 5:8

"If you are willing and obedient,
   You shall eat the good of the land;
   But if you refuse and rebel,
   You shall be devoured by the sword";
   For the mouth of the Lord has spoken.

ISAIAH 1:19–20

Therefore submit yourselves to every ordinance of man for the Lord's sake, whether to the king as supreme, or to governors, as to those who are sent by him for the punishment of evildoers and for the praise of those who do good. For this is the will of God, that by doing good you may put to silence the ignorance of foolish men.

1 PETER 2:13–15

Likewise you younger people, submit yourselves to your elders. Yes, all of you be submissive to one another, and be clothed with humility, for
   "God resists the proud,
     But gives grace to the humble."
   Therefore humble yourselves under the mighty hand of God, that he may exalt you in due time.

1 PETER 5:5–6

Let this mind be in you which was also in Christ Jesus, who, being in the form of God, did not consider it robbery to be equal with God, but made Himself of no reputation, taking the form of a bondservant, and coming in the likeness of men. And being found in appearance as a man, He humbled Himself and became obedient to the point of death, even the death of the cross.

PHILIPPIANS 2:5–8

Therefore do not let sin reign in your mortal body, that you should obey it in its lusts. And do not present your members as instruments of unrighteousness to sin, but present yourselves to God as being alive from the dead, and your members as instruments of righteousness to God.

ROMANS 6:12–13

This I say, therefore, and testify in the Lord, that you should no longer walk as the rest of the Gentiles walk, in the futility of their mind, having their understanding darkened, being alienated from the life of God, because of the ignorance that is in them, because of the blindness of their heart.

EPHESIANS 4:17–18

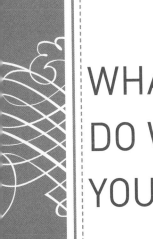

# WHAT TO
# DO WHEN
# YOU ARE . . .

# EXPERIENCING FEAR

For God has not given us a spirit of fear, but of power and of love and of a sound mind.

2 TIMOTHY 1:7

For you did not receive the spirit of bondage again to fear, but you received the Spirit of adoption by whom we cry out, "Abba, Father."

ROMANS 8:15

He shall cover you with His feathers,
    And under His wings you shall take refuge;
    His truth shall be your shield and buckler.
    You shall not be afraid of the terror by night,
    Nor of the arrow that flies by day,
    Nor of the pestilence that walks in darkness,
    Nor of the destruction that lays waste at noonday.
A thousand may fall at your side,
    And ten thousand at your right hand;
    But it shall not come near you.

PSALM 91:4–7

No evil shall befall you,
　Nor shall any plague come near your dwelling;
　For He shall give his angels charge over you,
　To keep you in all your ways.

PSALM 91:10–11

Do not be afraid of sudden terror,
　Nor of trouble from the wicked when it comes;
　For the LORD will be your confidence,
　And will keep your foot from being caught.

PROVERBS 3:25–26

In righteousness you shall be established;
　You shall be far from oppression, for you shall not
　　fear;
　And from terror, for it shall not come near you.

ISAIAH 54:14

In God I have put my trust;
　I will not be afraid.
　What can man do to me?

PSALM 56:11

There is no fear in love; but perfect love casts out fear, because fear involves torment. But he who fears has not been made perfect in love.

1 JOHN 4:18

He who dwells in the secret place of the Most High
Shall abide under the shadow of the Almighty.

PSALM 91:1

Yea, though I walk through the valley of the shadow
        of death,
    I will fear no evil;
    For You are with me;
    Your rod and Your staff, they comfort me.
You prepare a table before me in the presence of
        my enemies;
    You anoint my head with oil;
    My cup runs over.

PSALM 23:4–5

Peace I leave with you, My peace I give to you; not as the world gives do I give to you. Let not your heart be troubled, neither let it be afraid.

JOHN 14:27

Be of good courage,
    And He shall strengthen your heart,
    All you who hope in the LORD.

PSALM 31:24

The LORD is my light and my salvation;
    Whom shall I fear?
    The LORD is the strength of my life;
    Of whom shall I be afraid? . . .
    Though an army may encamp against me,
    My heart shall not fear;
    Though war may rise against me,
    In this I will be confident.

PSALM 27:1, 3

So we may boldly say:
    "The LORD is my helper;
    I will not fear.
    What can man do to me?"

HEBREWS 13:6

Who shall separate us from the love of Christ? Shall tribulation, or distress, or persecution, or famine, or nakedness, or peril, or sword? As it is written:

"For Your sake we are killed all day long;

We are accounted as sheep for the slaughter."

Yet in all these things we are more than conquerors through Him who loved us. For I am persuaded that neither death nor life, nor angels nor principalities nor powers, nor things present nor things to come, nor height nor depth, nor any other created thing, shall be able to separate us from the love of God which is in Christ Jesus our Lord.

ROMANS 8:35–39

# IN NEED OF FELLOWSHIP

For God has not given us a spirit of fear, but of power and of love and of a sound mind.

2 TIMOTHY 1:7

Fear not, for I am with you;
Be not dismayed, for I am your God.
I will strengthen you,
Yes, I will help you,
I will uphold you with My righteous right hand.

ISAIAH 41:10

For where envy and self-seeking exist, confusion and every evil thing are there. But the wisdom that is from above is first pure, then peaceable, gentle, willing to yield, full of mercy and good fruits, without partiality and without hypocrisy. Now the fruit of righteousness is sown in peace by those who make peace.

JAMES 3:16–18

Cast your burden on the LORD,
    And He shall sustain you;
    He shall never permit the righteous to be moved.

PSALM 55:22

For the Lord GOD will help Me;
    Therefore I will not be disgraced;
    Therefore I have set My face like a flint,
    And I know that I will not be ashamed.

ISAIAH 50:7

Be anxious for nothing, but in everything by prayer and supplication, with thanksgiving, let your requests be made known to God; and the peace of God, which surpasses all understanding, will guard your hearts and minds through Christ Jesus.

PHILIPPIANS 4:6–7

Therefore it is also contained in the Scripture,
    "Behold, I lay in Zion
    A chief cornerstone, elect, precious,
    And he who believes on Him will by no means be
        put to shame."

1 PETER 2:6

Great peace have those who love Your law,
And nothing causes them to stumble.

PSALM 119:165

When you pass through the waters, I will be with
you;
And through the rivers, they shall not overflow
you.
When you walk through the fire, you shall not be
burned,
Nor shall the flame scorch you.

ISAIAH 43:2

He heals the brokenhearted
And binds up their wounds.

PSALM 147:3

Blessed be the God and Father of our Lord Jesus
Christ, the Father of mercies and God of all comfort,
who comforts us in all our tribulation, that we may
be able to comfort those who are in any trouble, with
the comfort with which we ourselves are comforted
by God.

2 CORINTHIANS 1:3–4

Finally, brethren, whatever things are true, whatever things are noble, whatever things are just, whatever things are pure, whatever things are lovely, whatever things are of good report, if there is any virtue and if there is anything praiseworthy—meditate on these things.

PHILIPPIANS 4:8

For God is not the author of confusion but of peace.

1 CORINTHIANS 14:33

For I am persuaded that neither death nor life, nor angels nor principalities nor powers, nor things present nor things to come, nor height nor depth, nor any other created thing, shall be able to separate us from the love of God which is in Christ Jesus our Lord.

ROMANS 8:38–39

WHAT TO DO WHEN YOU ARE . . .

# IN NEED OF COURAGE

Wait on the LORD;
    Be of good courage,
    And He shall strengthen your heart;
    Wait, I say, on the LORD!

                  PSALM 27:14

I shall not die, but live,
    And declare the works of the LORD.

                  PSALM 118:17

For His anger is but for a moment,
    His favor is for life;
    Weeping may endure for a night,
    But joy comes in the morning.

                  PSALM 30:5

Be of good courage,
    And he shall strengthen your heart,
    All you who hope in the LORD.

                  PSALM 31:24

When you pass through the waters, I will be with you;
    And through the rivers, they shall not overflow you.
    When you walk through the fire, you shall not
        be burned,
Nor shall the flame scorch you.

ISAIAH 43:2

I can do all things through Christ who strengthens me.

PHILIPPIANS 4:13

Beloved, do not think it strange concerning the fiery trial which is to try you, as though some strange thing happened to you; but rejoice to the extent that you partake of Christ's sufferings, that when His glory is revealed, you may also be glad with exceeding joy.

1 PETER 4:12–13

For I am persuaded that neither death nor life, nor angels nor principalities nor powers, nor things present nor things to come, nor height nor depth, nor any other created thing, shall be able to separate us from the love of God which is in Christ Jesus our Lord.

ROMANS 8:38–39

Fear not, for I am with you;
    Be not dismayed, for I am your God.
    I will strengthen you,
    Yes, I will help you,
    I will uphold you with My righteous right hand.

ISAIAH 41:10

The eternal God is your refuge,
    And underneath are the everlasting arms;
    He will thrust out the enemy from before you,
    And will say, "Destroy!"

DEUTERONOMY 33:27

But those who wait on the LORD
    Shall renew their strength;
    They shall mount up with wings like eagles,
    They shall run and not be weary,
    They shall walk and not faint.

ISAIAH 40:31

Be anxious for nothing, but in everything by prayer and supplication, with thanksgiving, let your requests be made known to God.

PHILIPPIANS 4:6

Finally, brethren, whatever things are true, whatever things are noble, whatever things are just, whatever things are pure, whatever things are lovely, whatever things are of good report, if there is any virtue and if there is anything praiseworthy—meditate on these things.

PHILIPPIANS 4:8

So the ransomed of the Lord shall return,
    And come to Zion with singing,
    With everlasting joy on their heads.
    They shall obtain joy and gladness;
    Sorrow and sighing shall flee away.

ISAIAH 51:11

WHAT TO DO WHEN YOU ARE . . .

# IN NEED OF PATIENCE

But the fruit of the Spirit is love, joy, peace, longsuffering, kindness, goodness, faithfulness.

GALATIANS 5:22

But those who wait on the LORD
    Shall renew their strength;
    They shall mount up with wings like eagles,
    They shall run and not be weary,
    They shall walk and not faint.

ISAIAH 40:31

Wait on the LORD;
    Be of good courage,
    And He shall strengthen your heart;
    Wait, I say, on the LORD!

PSALM 27:14

It is good that one should hope and wait quietly
    For the salvation of the LORD.

LAMENTATIONS 3:26

But if we hope for what we do not see, we eagerly wait for it with perseverance.

ROMANS 8:25

Rest in the LORD, and wait patiently for Him;
>Do not fret because of him who prospers in
>>his way,
>Because of the man who brings wicked schemes
>>to pass.

PSALM 37:7

That you do not become sluggish, but imitate those who through faith and patience inherit the promises.

HEBREWS 6:12

Therefore do not cast away your confidence, which has great reward. For you have need of endurance, so that after you have done the will of God, you may receive the promise:
>"For yet a little while,
>And He who is coming will come and will not
>>tarry."

HEBREWS 10:35–37

I waited patiently for the LORD;
    And He inclined to me,
    And heard my cry.

PSALM 40:1

The end of a thing is better than its beginning;
    The patient in spirit is better than the proud
        in spirit.
    Do not hasten in your spirit to be angry,
    For anger rests in the bosom of fools.

ECCLESIASTES 7:8–9

For whatever things were written before were written for our learning, that we through the patience and comfort of the Scriptures might have hope. Now may the God of patience and comfort grant you to be like-minded toward one another, according to Christ Jesus.

ROMANS 15:4–5

Knowing that the testing of your faith produces patience. But let patience have its perfect work, that you may be perfect and complete, lacking nothing.

JAMES 1:3–4

Therefore we also, since we are surrounded by so great a cloud of witnesses, let us lay aside every weight, and the sin which so easily ensnares us, and let us run with endurance the race that is set before us.

HEBREWS 12:1

Cease from anger, and forsake wrath;
Do not fret—it only causes harm.
For evildoers shall be cut off;
But those who wait on the LORD,
They shall inherit the earth.

PSALM 37:8–9

Therefore be patient, brethren, until the coming of the Lord. See how the farmer waits for the precious fruit of the earth, waiting patiently for it until it receives the early and latter rain. You also be patient. Establish your hearts, for the coming of the Lord is at hand.

JAMES 5:7–8

# IN NEED OF PEACE

You will keep him in perfect peace,
Whose mind is stayed on You,
Because he trusts in You.

ISAIAH 26:3

Peace I leave with you, My peace I give to you; not as the world gives do I give to you. Let not your heart be troubled, neither let it be afraid.

JOHN 14:27

Be anxious for nothing, but in everything by prayer and supplication, with thanksgiving, let your requests be made known to God; and the peace of God, which surpasses all understanding, will guard your hearts and minds through Christ Jesus.

PHILIPPIANS 4:6–7

Therefore, having been justified by faith, we have peace with God through our Lord Jesus Christ.

ROMANS 5:1

LORD, You will establish peace for us,
    For You have also done all our works in us.

ISAIAH 26:12

For you shall go out with joy,
    And be led out with peace;
    The mountains and the hills
    Shall break forth into singing before you,
    And all the trees of the field shall clap their
        hands.

ISAIAH 55:12

For to be carnally minded is death, but to be spiritually minded is life and peace.

ROMANS 8:6

Mark the blameless man, and observe the upright;
    For the future of that man is peace.

PSALM 37:37

He shall enter into peace;
    They shall rest in their beds,
    Each one walking in his uprightness.

ISAIAH 57:2

For the kingdom of God is not eating and drinking, but righteousness and peace and joy in the Holy Spirit. For he who serves Christ in these things is acceptable to God and approved by men.

Therefore let us pursue the things which make for peace and the things by which one may edify another.

ROMANS 14:17–19

Great peace have those who love Your law,
And nothing causes them to stumble.

PSALM 119:165

But the meek shall inherit the earth,
And shall delight themselves in the abundance of
peace.

PSALM 37:11

Finally, brethren, farewell. Become complete. Be of good comfort, be of one mind, live in peace; and the God of love and peace will be with you.

2 CORINTHIANS 13:11

WHAT TO DO WHEN YOU ARE . . .

# LUKEWARM SPIRITUALLY

Be watchful, and strengthen the things which remain, that are ready to die, for I have not found your works perfect before God. . . .

I know your works, that you are neither cold nor hot. I could wish you were cold or hot. So then, because you are lukewarm, and neither cold nor hot, I will vomit you out of My mouth.

REVELATION 3:2, 15–16

O Ephraim, what shall I do to you?
O Judah, what shall I do to you?
For your faithfulness is like a morning cloud,
And like the early dew it goes away.

HOSEA 6:4

If we had forgotten the name of our God,
Or stretched out our hands to a foreign god,
Would not God search this out?
For He knows the secrets of the heart.

PSALM 44:20–21

Only take heed to yourself, and diligently keep yourself, lest you forget the things your eyes have seen, and lest they depart from your heart all the days of your life. And teach them to your children and your grandchildren.

DEUTERONOMY 4:9

Beware that you do not forget the LORD your God by not keeping His commandments, His judgments, and His statutes which I command you today, lest—when you have eaten and are full, and have built beautiful houses and dwell in them; and when your herds and your flocks multiply, and your silver and your gold are multiplied, and all that you have is multiplied; when your heart is lifted up, and you forget the LORD your God who brought you out of the land of Egypt, from the house of bondage.

DEUTERONOMY 8:11–14

If we confess our sins, He is faithful and just to forgive us our sins and to cleanse us from all unrighteousness.

1 JOHN 1:9

Of whom we have much to say, and hard to explain, since you have become dull of hearing.

For though by this time you ought to be teachers, you need someone to teach you again the first principles of the oracles of God; and you have come to need milk and not solid food.

HEBREWS 5:11–12

Beware, brethren, lest there be in any of you an evil heart of unbelief in departing from the living God; but exhort one another daily, while it is called "Today," lest any of you be hardened through the deceitfulness of sin.

HEBREWS 3:12–13

Looking carefully lest anyone fall short of the grace of God; lest any root of bitterness springing up cause trouble, and by this many become defiled.

HEBREWS 12:15

Nevertheless I have this against you, that you have left your first love.

REVELATION 2:4

Thus says the Lord:

"Stand in the ways and see,
And ask for the old paths, where the good way is,
And walk in it;
Then you will find rest for your souls.
But they said, 'We will not walk in it.' "

JEREMIAH 6:16

For if, after they have escaped the pollutions of the world through the knowledge of the Lord and Savior Jesus Christ, they are again entangled in them and overcome, the latter end is worse for them than the beginning. For it would have been better for them not to have known the way of righteousness, than having known it, to turn from the holy commandment delivered to them.

2 PETER 2:20–21

"Yet from the days of your fathers
You have gone away from My ordinances
And have not kept them.
Return to Me, and I will return to you,"
Says the Lord of hosts.

MALACHI 3:7

WHAT TO DO WHEN YOU ARE . . .

# IN GRIEF

But I do not want you to be ignorant, brethren, concerning those who have fallen asleep, lest you sorrow as others who have no hope. For if we believe that Jesus died and rose again, even so God will bring with Him those who sleep in Jesus.

1 THESSALONIANS 4:13–14

Now may our Lord Jesus Christ Himself, and our God and Father, who has loved us and given us everlasting consolation and good hope by grace, comfort your hearts and establish you in every good word and work.

2 THESSALONIANS 2:16–17

For the LORD has comforted His people,
   And will have mercy on His afflicted.

ISAIAH 49:13

When you pass through the waters, I will be
      with you;
   And through the rivers, they shall not
      overflow you.
   When you walk through the fire, you shall not
      be burned,
   Nor shall the flame scorch you.

ISAIAH 43:2

Blessed be the God and Father of our Lord Jesus Christ, the Father of mercies and God of all comfort, who comforts us in all our tribulation, that we may be able to comfort those who are in any trouble, with the comfort with which we ourselves are comforted by God.

2 CORINTHIANS 1:3–4

This is my comfort in my affliction,
   For Your word has given me life.

PSALM 119:50

Casting all your care upon Him, for He cares for you.

1 PETER 5:7

The Spirit of the Lord God is upon Me,
    Because the Lord has anointed Me
    To preach good tidings to the poor;
    He has sent Me to heal the brokenhearted,
    To proclaim liberty to the captives,
    And the opening of the prison to those who are
        bound;
    To proclaim the acceptable year of the Lord,
    And the day of vengeance of our God;
    To comfort all who mourn,
    To console those who mourn in Zion,
    To give them beauty for ashes,
    The oil of joy for mourning,
    The garment of praise for the spirit of heaviness;
    That they may be called trees of righteousness,
    The planting of the Lord, that He may be
        glorified.

ISAIAH 61:1–3

Blessed are those who mourn,
    For they shall be comforted.

MATTHEW 5:4

"O Death, where is your sting?
O Hades, where is your victory?"
The sting of death is sin, and the strength of sin is the law. But thanks be to God, who gives us the victory through our Lord Jesus Christ.

1 CORINTHIANS 15:55–57

Yea, though I walk through the valley of the shadow
of death,
I will fear no evil;
For You are with me;
Your rod and Your staff, they comfort me.

PSALM 23:4

We are confident, yes, well pleased rather to be absent from the body and to be present with the Lord.

2 CORINTHIANS 5:8

So the ransomed of the LORD shall return,
And come to Zion with singing,
With everlasting joy on their heads.
They shall obtain joy and gladness;
Sorrow and sighing shall flee away.

ISAIAH 51:11

For we do not have a High Priest who cannot sympathize with our weaknesses, but was in all points tempted as we are, yet without sin.

Let us therefore come boldly to the throne of grace, that we may obtain mercy and find grace to help in time of need.

HEBREWS 4:15–16

Fear not, for I am with you;
Be not dismayed, for I am your God.
I will strengthen you,
Yes, I will help you,
I will uphold you with My righteous right hand.

ISAIAH 41:10

And God will wipe away every tear from their eyes; there shall be no more death, nor sorrow, nor crying. There shall be no more pain, for the former things have passed away.

REVELATION 21:4

# IN DOUBT ABOUT GOD

So Jesus answered and said to them, "Have faith in God. For assuredly, I say to you, whoever says to this mountain, 'Be removed and be cast into the sea,' and does not doubt in his heart, but believes that those things he says will be done, he will have whatever he says. Therefore I say to you, whatever things you ask when you pray, believe that you receive them, and you will have them."

MARK 11:22–24

He did not waver at the promise of God through unbelief, but was strengthened in faith, giving glory to God, and being fully convinced that what He had promised He was also able to perform.

ROMANS 4:20–21

He who calls you is faithful, who also will do it.

1 THESSALONIANS 5:24

And do not seek what you should eat or what you should drink, nor have an anxious mind. For all these things the nations of the world seek after, and your Father knows that you need these things. But seek the kingdom of God, and all these things shall be added to you.

LUKE 12:29–31

My counsel shall stand,
   And I will do all My pleasure,
   Indeed I have spoken it;
   I will also bring it to pass.
   I have purposed it;
   I will also do it.

ISAIAH 46:10–11

The Lord is not slack concerning His promise, as some count slackness, but is longsuffering toward us, not willing that any should perish but that all should come to repentance.

2 PETER 3:9

Behold, the LORD's hand is not shortened,
That it cannot save;
Nor His ear heavy,
That it cannot hear.

ISAIAH 59:1

For as the rain comes down, and the snow from
heaven,
And do not return there,
But water the earth,
And make it bring forth and bud,
That it may give seed to the sower
And bread to the eater,
So shall My word be that goes forth from My
mouth;
It shall not return to Me void,
But it shall accomplish what I please,
And it shall prosper in the thing for which I sent it.

ISAIAH 55:10–11

So then faith comes by hearing, and hearing by the
word of God.

ROMANS 10:17

Beloved, do not think it strange concerning the fiery trial which is to try you, as though some strange thing happened to you; but rejoice to the extent that you partake of Christ's sufferings, that when His glory is revealed, you may also be glad with exceeding joy.

1 PETER 4:12–13

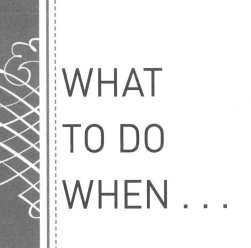

WHAT
TO DO
WHEN . . .

WHAT TO DO WHEN . . .

# YOU NEED CONFIDENCE

I can do all things through Christ who strengthens me.

PHILIPPIANS 4:13

So we may boldly say:
"The LORD is my helper;
I will not fear.
What can man do to me?"

HEBREWS 13:6

Therefore do not cast away your confidence, which has great reward. For you have need of endurance, so that after you have done the will of God, you may receive the promise.

HEBREWS 10:35–36

Being confident of this very thing, that He who has begun a good work in you will complete it until the day of Jesus Christ.

PHILIPPIANS 1:6

The Lord God is my strength;
   He will make my feet like deer's feet,
   And He will make me walk on my high hills.

HABAKKUK 3:19

Yet in all these things we are more than conquerors through Him who loved us.

ROMANS 8:37

Now this is the confidence that we have in Him, that if we ask anything according to His will, He hears us. And if we know that He hears us, whatever we ask, we know that we have the petitions that we have asked of Him.

1 JOHN 5:14–15

Most assuredly, I say to you, he who believes in Me, the works that I do he will do also; and greater works than these he will do, because I go to My Father.

JOHN 14:12

For the Lord will be your confidence,
   And will keep your foot from being caught.

PROVERBS 3:26

So he answered and said to me:

"This is the word of the LORD to Zerubbabel:
'Not by might nor by power, but by My Spirit,'
Says the LORD of hosts."

ZECHARIAH 4:6

When you pass through the waters, I will be with you;
And through the rivers, they shall not overflow
you.
When you walk through the fire, you shall not be
burned,
Nor shall the flame scorch you.

ISAIAH 43:2

In whom we have boldness and access with confidence through faith in Him.

EPHESIANS 3:12

But those who wait on the LORD
Shall renew their strength;
They shall mount up with wings like eagles,
They shall run and not be weary,
They shall walk and not faint.

ISAIAH 40:31

WHAT TO DO WHEN . . .

# TROUBLES HIT YOUR LIFE

The LORD is good,
A stronghold in the day of trouble;
And He knows those who trust in Him.

NAHUM 1:7

We are hard-pressed on every side, yet not crushed; we are perplexed, but not in despair; persecuted, but not forsaken; struck down, but not destroyed.

2 CORINTHIANS 4:8–9

Though I walk in the midst of trouble, You will
revive me;
You will stretch out Your hand
Against the wrath of my enemies,
And Your right hand will save me.

PSALM 138:7

Let not your heart be troubled; you believe in God, believe also in Me.

JOHN 14:1

And we know that all things work together for good to those who love God, to those who are the called according to His purpose.

ROMANS 8:28

I will be glad and rejoice in Your mercy,
For you have considered my trouble;
You have known my soul in adversities.

PSALM 31:7

I will lift up my eyes to the hills—
From whence comes my help?
My help comes from the LORD,
Who made heaven and earth.

PSALM 121:1–2

For we do not have a High Priest who cannot sympathize with our weaknesses, but was in all points tempted as we are, yet without sin. Let us therefore come boldly to the throne of grace, that we may obtain mercy and find grace to help in time of need.

HEBREWS 4:15–16

Casting all your care upon Him, for He cares for you.

1 PETER 5:7

Therefore do not worry about tomorrow, for tomorrow will worry about its own things. Sufficient for the day is its own trouble.

MATTHEW 6:34

Blessed be the God and Father of our Lord Jesus Christ, the Father of mercies and God of all comfort, who comforts us in all our tribulation, that we may be able to comfort those who are in any trouble, with the comfort with which we ourselves are comforted by God.

2 CORINTHIANS 1:3–4

Be anxious for nothing, but in everything by prayer and supplication, with thanksgiving, let your requests be made known to God; and the peace of God, which surpasses all understanding, will guard your hearts and minds through Christ Jesus.

PHILIPPIANS 4:6–7

# YOU HAVE A PHYSICAL SICKNESS

Beloved, I pray that you may prosper in all things and be in health, just as your soul prospers.

3 JOHN V. 2

Then Jesus went about all the cities and villages, teaching in their synagogues, preaching the gospel of the kingdom, and healing every sickness and every disease among the people.

MATTHEW 9:35

And the whole multitude sought to touch Him, for power went out from Him and healed them all.

LUKE 6:19

Jesus Christ is the same yesterday, today, and forever.

HEBREWS 13:8

Who Himself bore our sins in His own body on the tree, that we, having died to sins, might live for righteousness—by whose stripes you were healed.

1 PETER 2:24

Who forgives all your iniquities,
Who heals all your diseases.

PSALM 103:3

But He was wounded for our transgressions,
He was bruised for our iniquities;
The chastisement for our peace was upon Him,
And by His stripes we are healed.

ISAIAH 53:5

My son, give attention to my words;
Incline your ear to my sayings.
Do not let them depart from your eyes;
Keep them in the midst of your heart;
For they are life to those who find them,
And health to all their flesh.

PROVERBS 4:20–22

Is anyone among you sick? Let him call for the elders of the church, and let them pray over him, anointing him with oil in the name of the Lord. And the prayer of faith will save the sick, and the Lord will raise him up. And if he has committed sins, he will be forgiven.

JAMES 5:14–15

If you diligently heed the voice of the Lord your God and do what is right in His sight, give ear to His commandments and keep all His statutes, I will put none of the diseases on you which I have brought on the Egyptians. For I am the Lord who heals you.

EXODUS 15:26

"For I will restore health to you
    And heal you of your wounds," says the Lord.

JEREMIAH 30:17

Heal me, O Lord, and I shall be healed;
    Save me, and I shall be saved,
    For You are my praise.

JEREMIAH 17:14

The centurion answered and said, "Lord, I am not worthy that You should come under my roof. But only speak a word, and my servant will be healed."

MATTHEW 8:8

He sent His word and healed them,
And delivered them from their destructions.

PSALM 107:20

And these signs will follow those who believe: In My name they will cast out demons; they will speak with new tongues; they will take up serpents; and if they drink anything deadly, it will by no means hurt them; they will lay hands on the sick, and they will recover.

MARK 16:17–18

WHAT TO DO WHEN . . .

# YOU ARE IN
# FINANCIAL TROUBLE

---

Beloved, I pray that you may prosper in all things and be in health, just as your soul prospers.

3 JOHN V. 2

I have been young, and now am old;
    Yet I have not seen the righteous forsaken,
    Nor his descendants begging bread.

PSALM 37:25

The young lions lack and suffer hunger;
    But those who seek the LORD shall not lack any
        good thing.

PSALM 34:10

The LORD is my shepherd;
    I shall not want.

PSALM 23:1

And all these blessings shall come upon you and overtake you, because you obey the voice of the LORD your God:

"Blessed shall you be in the city, and blessed shall you be in the country.

"Blessed shall be the fruit of your body, the produce of your ground and the increase of your herds, the increase of your cattle and the offspring of your flocks.

"Blessed shall be your basket and your kneading bowl.

"Blessed shall you be when you come in, and blessed shall you be when you go out.

"The LORD will cause your enemies who rise against you to be defeated before your face; they shall come out against you one way and flee before you seven ways.

"The LORD will command the blessing on you in your storehouses and in all to which you set your hand, and He will bless you in the land which the LORD your God is giving you."

DEUTERONOMY 28:2–8

And the Lord will grant you plenty of goods, in the fruit of your body, in the increase of your livestock, and in the produce of your ground, in the land of which the Lord swore to your fathers to give you. The Lord will open to you His good treasure, the heavens, to give the rain to your land in its season, and to bless all the work of your hand. You shall lend to many nations, but you shall not borrow. And the Lord will make you the head and not the tail; you shall be above only, and not be beneath, if you heed the commandments of the Lord your God, which I command you today, and are careful to observe them.

DEUTERONOMY 28:11–13

Give, and it will be given to you: good measure, pressed down, shaken together, and running over will be put into your bosom. For with the same measure that you use, it will be measured back to you.

LUKE 6:38

On the first day of the week let each one of you lay something aside, storing up as he may prosper, that there be no collections when I come.

1 CORINTHIANS 16:2

"Bring all the tithes into the storehouse,
That there may be food in My house,
And try Me now in this,"
Says the Lord of hosts,
"If I will not open for you the windows of heaven
And pour out for you such blessing
That there will not be room enough to receive it.
"And I will rebuke the devourer for your sakes,
So that he will not destroy the fruit of your
ground,
Nor shall the vine fail to bear fruit for you in
the field,"
Says the Lord of hosts;
"And all nations will call you blessed,
For you will be a delightful land,"
Says the Lord of hosts.

MALACHI 3:10–12

And everyone who has left houses or brothers or sisters or father or mother or wife or children or lands, for My name's sake, shall receive a hundredfold, and inherit eternal life.

MATTHEW 19:29

But this I say: He who sows sparingly will also reap sparingly, and he who sows bountifully will also reap bountifully. So let each one give as he purposes in his heart, not grudgingly or of necessity; for God loves a cheerful giver. And God is able to make all grace abound toward you, that you, always having all sufficiency in all things, may have an abundance for every good work.

2 CORINTHIANS 9:6–8

Heal the sick, cleanse the lepers, raise the dead, cast out demons. Freely you have received, freely give.

MATTHEW 10:8

And my God shall supply all your need according to His riches in glory by Christ Jesus.

PHILIPPIANS 4:19

A good man leaves an inheritance to his children's children,
    But the wealth of the sinner is stored up for the righteous.

PROVERBS 13:22

This Book of the Law shall not depart from your mouth, but you shall meditate in it day and night, that you may observe to do according to all that is written in it. For then you will make your way prosperous, and then you will have good success.

JOSHUA 1:8

For God gives wisdom and knowledge and joy to a man who is good in His sight; but to the sinner He gives the work of gathering and collecting, that he may give to him who is good before God. This also is vanity and grasping for the wind.

ECCLESIASTES 2:26

Therefore do not worry, saying, "What shall we eat?" or "What shall we drink?" or "What shall we wear?" For after all these things the Gentiles seek. For your heavenly Father knows that you need all these things. But seek first the kingdom of God and His righteousness, and all these things shall be added to you.

MATTHEW 6:31–33

For the LORD your God is bringing you into a good land, a land of brooks of water, of fountains and springs, that flow out of valleys and hills; a land of wheat and barley, of vines and fig trees and pomegranates, a land of olive oil and honey; a land in which you will eat bread without scarcity, in which you will lack nothing; a land whose stones are iron and out of whose hills you can dig copper. When you have eaten and are full, then you shall bless the LORD your God for the good land which He has given you. . . .

And you shall remember the LORD your God, for it is he who gives you power to get wealth, that He may establish His covenant which He swore to your fathers, as it is this day.

DEUTERONOMY 8:7–10, 18

# YOU ARE HAVING MARITAL PROBLEMS

Let all bitterness, wrath, anger, clamor, and evil speaking be put away from you, with all malice. And be kind to one another, tenderhearted, forgiving one another, even as God in Christ forgave you.

EPHESIANS 4:31–32

And the Lord God said, "It is not good that man should be alone; I will make him a helper comparable to him."

GENESIS 2:18

Therefore a man shall leave his father and mother and be joined to his wife, and they shall become one flesh.

GENESIS 2:24

Hatred stirs up strife,
But love covers all sins.

PROVERBS 10:12

Submitting to one another in the fear of God.

Wives, submit to your own husbands, as to the Lord. For the husband is head of the wife, as also Christ is head of the church; and He is the Savior of the body. Therefore, just as the church is subject to Christ, so let the wives be to their own husbands in everything.

Husbands, love your wives, just as Christ also loved the church and gave Himself for her, that He might sanctify and cleanse her with the washing of water by the word, that He might present her to Himself a glorious church, not having spot or wrinkle or any such thing, but that she should be holy and without blemish. So husbands ought to love their own wives as their own bodies; he who loves his wife loves himself. For no one ever hated his own flesh, but nourishes and cherishes it, just as the Lord does the church. For we are members of His body, of His flesh and of His bones. "For this reason a man shall leave his father and mother and be joined to his wife, and the two shall become one flesh." This is a great mystery, but I speak concerning Christ and the church. Nevertheless let each one of you in particular so love his own wife as himself, and let the wife see that she respects her husband.

EPHESIANS 5:21–33

I will behave wisely in a perfect way.
Oh, when will You come to me?
I will walk within my house with a perfect heart.

PSALM 101:2

And if it seems evil to you to serve the LORD, choose for yourselves this day whom you will serve, whether the gods which your fathers served that were on the other side of the River, or the gods of the Amorites, in whose land you dwell. But as for me and my house, we will serve the LORD.

JOSHUA 24:15

Love does no harm to a neighbor; therefore love is the fulfillment of the law.

ROMANS 13:10

Wives, likewise, be submissive to your own husbands, that even if some do not obey the word, they, without a word, may be won by the conduct of their wives, when they observe your chaste conduct accompanied by fear. Do not let your adornment be merely outward—arranging the hair, wearing gold, or putting on fine apparel—rather let it be the hidden person of the heart, with the incorruptible beauty of a gentle and quiet spirit, which is very precious in the sight of God. For in this manner, in former times, the holy women who trusted in God also adorned themselves, being submissive to their own husbands, as Sarah obeyed Abraham, calling him lord, whose daughters you are if you do good and are not afraid with any terror.

Husbands, likewise, dwell with them with understanding, giving honor to the wife, as to the weaker vessel, and as being heirs together of the grace of life, that your prayers may not be hindered.

1 PETER 3:1–7

Finally, all of you be of one mind, having compassion for one another; love as brothers, be tenderhearted, be courteous; not returning evil for evil or reviling for reviling, but on the contrary blessing, knowing that you were called to this, that you may inherit a blessing. For

"He who would love life
And see good days,
Let him refrain his tongue from evil,
And his lips from speaking deceit.
Let him turn away from evil and do good;
Let him seek peace and pursue it."

1 PETER 3:8–11

Trust in the LORD with all your heart,
And lean not on your own understanding;
In all your ways acknowledge Him,
And He shall direct your paths.

PROVERBS 3:5–6

Since you have purified your souls in obeying the truth through the Spirit in sincere love of the brethren, love one another fervently with a pure heart.

1 PETER 1:22

# YOU ARE DESERTED BY LOVED ONES

---

And those who know Your name will put their trust
     in You;
  For You, Lord, have not forsaken those who
      seek You.

PSALM 9:10

(For the Lord your God is a merciful God), He will not
forsake you nor destroy you, nor forget the covenant
of your fathers which He swore to them.

DEUTERONOMY 4:31

For the Lord will not cast off His people,
  Nor will He forsake His inheritance.

PSALM 94:14

When my father and my mother forsake me,
  Then the Lord will take care of me.

PSALM 27:10

Teaching them to observe all things that I have commanded you; and lo, I am with you always, even to the end of the age. Amen.

MATTHEW 28:20

You shall no longer be termed Forsaken,
    Nor shall your land any more be termed Desolate;
    But you shall be called Hephzibah, and your land
        Beulah;
    For the LORD delights in you,
    And your land shall be married.

ISAIAH 62:4

Persecuted, but not forsaken; struck down, but not destroyed.

2 CORINTHIANS 4:9

The poor and needy seek water, but there is none,
    Their tongues fail for thirst.
    I, the LORD, will hear them;
    I, the God of Israel, will not forsake them.

ISAIAH 41:17

Because he has set his love upon Me, therefore I
    will deliver him;
  I will set him on high, because he has known My
    name.
  He shall call upon Me, and I will answer him;
  I will be with him in trouble;
  I will deliver him and honor him.

PSALM 91:14–15

I have been young, and now am old;
  Yet I have not seen the righteous forsaken,
  Nor his descendants begging bread.

PSALM 37:25

Can a woman forget her nursing child,
  And not have compassion on the son of her
    womb?
  Surely they may forget,
  Yet I will not forget you.
  See, I have inscribed you on the palms of My
    hands;
  Your walls are continually before Me.

ISAIAH 49:15–16

Be strong and of good courage, do not fear nor be afraid of them; for the LORD your God, He is the One who goes with you. He will not leave you nor forsake you.

DEUTERONOMY 31:6

Why are you cast down, O my soul?
  And why are you disquieted within me?
  Hope in God;
  For I shall yet praise Him,
  The help of my countenance and my God.

PSALM 43:5

For the LORD will not forsake His people, for His great name's sake, because it has pleased the LORD to make you His people.

1 SAMUEL 12:22

Casting all your care upon Him, for He cares for you.

1 PETER 5:7

# YOU DO NOT UNDERSTAND GOD'S WAYS

"For My thoughts are not your thoughts,
Nor are your ways My ways," says the LORD.
"For as the heavens are higher than the earth,
So are My ways higher than your ways,
And My thoughts than your thoughts."

ISAIAH 55:8–9

Call to Me, and I will answer you, and show you great and mighty things, which you do not know.

JEREMIAH 33:3

What then shall we say to these things? If God is for us, who can be against us?

ROMANS 8:31

Many are the afflictions of the righteous,
But the LORD delivers him out of them all.

PSALM 34:19

Who shall separate us from the love of Christ? Shall tribulation, or distress, or persecution, or famine, or nakedness, or peril, or sword? As it is written:

"For Your sake we are killed all day long;

We are accounted as sheep for the slaughter."

Yet in all these things we are more than conquerors through Him who loved us.

ROMANS 8:35–37

No temptation has overtaken you except such as is common to man; but God is faithful, who will not allow you to be tempted beyond what you are able, but with the temptation will also make the way of escape, that you may be able to bear it.

1 CORINTHIANS 10:13

Fear not, for I am with you;

Be not dismayed, for I am your God.

I will strengthen you,

Yes, I will help you,

I will uphold you with My righteous right hand.

ISAIAH 41:10

And we know that all things work together for good

to those who love God, to those who are the called according to His purpose.

ROMANS 8:28

As for God, His way is perfect;
    The word of the LORD is proven;
    He is a shield to all who trust in Him.

PSALM 18:30

Let us know,
    Let us pursue the knowledge of the LORD.
    His going forth is established as the morning;
    He will come to us like the rain,
    Like the latter and former rain to the earth.

HOSEA 6:3

And I will make an everlasting covenant with them, that I will not turn away from doing them good; but I will put My fear in their hearts so that they will not depart from Me.

JEREMIAH 32:40

Cast your burden on the LORD,
 And He shall sustain you;
 He shall never permit the righteous to be moved.

PSALM 55:22

Let us hold fast the confession of our hope without wavering, for He who promised is faithful.

HEBREWS 10:23

The LORD will perfect that which concerns me;
 Your mercy, O LORD, endures forever;
 Do not forsake the works of Your hands.

PSALM 138:8

Beloved, do not think it strange concerning the fiery trial which is to try you, as though some strange thing happened to you; but rejoice to the extent that you partake of Christ's sufferings, that when His glory is revealed, you may also be glad with exceeding joy.

1 PETER 4:12–13

WHAT TO DO WHEN . . .

# YOU ARE WAITING ON GOD

Wait on the LORD;
    Be of good courage,
    And He shall strengthen your heart;
    Wait, I say, on the LORD!

PSALM 27:14

My soul, wait silently for God alone,
    For my expectation is from Him.

PSALM 62:5

Our soul waits for the LORD;
    He is our help and our shield.

PSALM 33:20

Let us hold fast the confession of our hope without wavering, for He who promised is faithful.

HEBREWS 10:23

But those who wait on the LORD
>   Shall renew their strength;
>   They shall mount up with wings like eagles,
>   They shall run and not be weary,
>   They shall walk and not faint.

ISAIAH 40:31

For the vision is yet for an appointed time;
>   But at the end it will speak, and it will not lie.
>   Though it tarries, wait for it;
>   Because it will surely come,
>   It will not tarry.

HABAKKUK 2:3

For we have become partakers of Christ if we hold the beginning of our confidence steadfast to the end.

HEBREWS 3:14

The eyes of all look expectantly to You,
>   And You give them their food in due season.
>   You open Your hand
>   And satisfy the desire of every living thing.

PSALM 145:15–16

I wait for the LORD, my soul waits,
And in His word I do hope.

PSALM 130:5

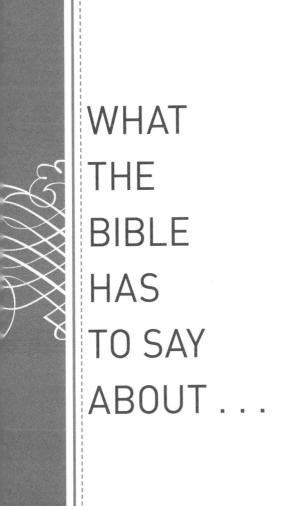

WHAT
THE
BIBLE
HAS
TO SAY
ABOUT . . .

# FAITH

Now faith is the substance of things hoped for, the evidence of things not seen.

HEBREWS 11:1

So then faith comes by hearing, and hearing by the word of God.

ROMANS 10:17

For I say, through the grace given to me, to everyone who is among you, not to think of himself more highly than he ought to think, but to think soberly, as God has dealt to each one a measure of faith.

ROMANS 12:3

Looking unto Jesus, the author and finisher of our faith, who for the joy that was set before Him endured the cross, despising the shame, and has sat down at the right hand of the throne of God.

HEBREWS 12:2

So Jesus said to them, "Because of your unbelief; for assuredly, I say to you, if you have faith as a mustard seed, you will say to this mountain, 'Move from here to there,' and it will move; and nothing will be impossible for you."

MATTHEW 17:20

So Jesus answered and said to them, "Have faith in God. For assuredly, I say to you, whoever says to this mountain, 'Be removed and be cast into the sea,' and does not doubt in his heart, but believes that those things he says will be done, he will have whatever he says. Therefore I say to you, whatever things you ask when you pray, believe that you receive them, and you will have them."

MARK 11:22–24

For in it the righteousness of God is revealed from faith to faith; as it is written, "The just shall live by faith."

ROMANS 1:17

For we walk by faith, not by sight.

2 CORINTHIANS 5:7

But without faith it is impossible to please Him, for he who comes to God must believe that He is, and that He is a rewarder of those who diligently seek Him.

HEBREWS 11:6

That the genuineness of your faith, being much more precious than gold that perishes, though it is tested by fire, may be found to praise, honor, and glory at the revelation of Jesus Christ, whom having not seen you love. Though now you do not see Him, yet believing, you rejoice with joy inexpressible and full of glory, receiving the end of your faith—the salvation of your souls.

1 PETER 1:7–9

For whatever is born of God overcomes the world. And this is the victory that has overcome the world—our faith.

1 JOHN 5:4

And suddenly, a woman who had a flow of blood for twelve years came from behind and touched the hem of His garment. For she said to herself, "If only I may touch His garment, I shall be made well." But Jesus turned around, and when He saw her He said, "Be of good cheer, daughter; your faith has made you well." And the woman was made well from that hour.

MATTHEW 9:20–22

And when He had come into the house, the blind men came to Him. And Jesus said to them, "Do you believe that I am able to do this?"

They said to Him, "Yes, Lord."

Then He touched their eyes, saying, "According to your faith let it be to you."

MATTHEW 9:28–29

Jesus said to him, "If you can believe, all things are possible to him who believes."

MARK 9:23

Is anyone among you sick? Let him call for the elders of the church, and let them pray over him, anointing him with oil in the name of the Lord. And the prayer of faith will save the sick, and the Lord will raise him up.

JAMES 5:14–15

WHAT THE BIBLE HAS TO SAY ABOUT . . .

# LOVE

---

Beloved, let us love one another, for love is of God; and everyone who loves is born of God and knows God. He who does not love does not know God, for God is love.

1 JOHN 4:7–8

In this is love, not that we loved God, but that He loved us and sent His Son to be the propitiation for our sins. Beloved, if God so loved us, we also ought to love one another.

No one has seen God at any time. If we love one another, God abides in us, and His love has been perfected in us.

1 JOHN 4:10–12

As the Father loved Me, I also have loved you; abide in My love. If you keep My commandments, you will abide in My love, just as I have kept My Father's commandments and abide in His love.

JOHN 15:9–10

Though I speak with the tongues of men and of angels, but have not love, I have become sounding brass or a clanging cymbal. And though I have the gift of prophecy, and understand all mysteries and all knowledge, and though I have all faith, so that I could remove mountains, but have not love, I am nothing. And though I bestow all my goods to feed the poor, and though I give my body to be burned, but have not love, it profits me nothing.

Love suffers long and is kind; love does not envy; love does not parade itself, is not puffed up; does not behave rudely, does not seek its own, is not provoked, thinks no evil; does not rejoice in iniquity, but rejoices in the truth; bears all things, believes all things, hopes all things, endures all things.

Love never fails. . . .

And now abide faith, hope, love, these three; but the greatest of these is love.

1 CORINTHIANS 13:1–8, 13

But God demonstrates His own love toward us, in that while we were still sinners, Christ died for us.

ROMANS 5:8

This is My commandment, that you love one another as I have loved you. Greater love has no one than this, than to lay down one's life for his friends. You are My friends if you do whatever I command you. . . .

These things I command you, that you love one another.

JOHN 15:12–14, 17

"And you shall love the Lord your God with all your heart, with all your soul, with all your mind, and with all your strength." This is the first commandment. And the second, like it, is this: "You shall love your neighbor as yourself." There is no other commandment greater than these. . . .

And to love Him with all the heart, with all the understanding, with all the soul, and with all the strength, and to love one's neighbor as oneself, is more than all the whole burnt offerings and sacrifices.

MARK 12:30–31, 33

For the Father Himself loves you, because you have loved Me, and have believed that I came forth from God.

JOHN 16:27

And we have known and believed the love that God has for us. God is love, and he who abides in love abides in God, and God in him. . . .

And this commandment we have from Him: that he who loves God must love his brother also.

1 JOHN 4:16, 21

He who has My commandments and keeps them, it is he who loves Me. And he who loves Me will be loved by My Father, and I will love him and manifest Myself to him.

JOHN 14:21

The LORD has appeared of old to me, saying:
   "Yes, I have loved you with an everlasting love;
   Therefore with lovingkindness I have drawn you."

JEREMIAH 31:3

For God so loved the world that He gave His only begotten Son, that whoever believes in Him should not perish but have everlasting life.

JOHN 3:16

For I am persuaded that neither death nor life, nor angels nor principalities nor powers, nor things present nor things to come, nor height nor depth, nor any other created thing, shall be able to separate us from the love of God which is in Christ Jesus our Lord.

ROMANS 8:38–39

A new commandment I give to you, that you love one another; as I have loved you, that you also love one another. By this all will know that you are My disciples, if you have love for one another.

JOHN 13:34–35

WHAT THE BIBLE HAS TO SAY ABOUT . . .

# ETERNITY

And this is the testimony: that God has given us eternal life, and this life is in His Son.

1 JOHN 5:11

Most assuredly, I say to you, he who hears My word and believes in Him who sent Me has everlasting life, and shall not come into judgment, but has passed from death into life.

JOHN 5:24

For God so loved the world that He gave His only begotten Son, that whoever believes in Him should not perish but have everlasting life.

JOHN 3:16

Most assuredly, I say to you, he who believes in Me has everlasting life.

JOHN 6:47

And we know that the Son of God has come and has given us an understanding, that we may know Him who is true; and we are in Him who is true, in His Son Jesus Christ. This is the true God and eternal life.

1 JOHN 5:20

I am the living bread which came down from heaven. If anyone eats of this bread, he will live forever; and the bread that I shall give is My flesh, which I shall give for the life of the world.

JOHN 6:51

The poor shall eat and be satisfied;
    Those who seek Him will praise the LORD.
    Let your heart live forever!

PSALM 22:26

Surely goodness and mercy shall follow me
    All the days of my life;
    And I will dwell in the house of the LORD
    Forever.

PSALM 23:6

But God will redeem my soul from the power of
        the grave,
    For He shall receive me. Selah

PSALM 49:15

So when this corruptible has put on incorruption,
and this mortal has put on immortality, then shall be
brought to pass the saying that is written: "Death is
swallowed up in victory."
    "O Death, where is your sting?
    O Hades, where is your victory?"

1 CORINTHIANS 15:54–55

Jesus said to her, "I am the resurrection and the
life. He who believes in Me, though he may die, he
shall live. And whoever lives and believes in Me shall
never die. Do you believe this?"

JOHN 11:25–26

Do not labor for the food which perishes, but for the
food which endures to everlasting life, which the Son
of Man will give you, because God the Father has set
His seal on Him.

JOHN 6:27

My sheep hear My voice, and I know them, and they follow Me. And I give them eternal life, and they shall never perish; neither shall anyone snatch them out of My hand.

JOHN 10:27–28

The LORD knows the days of the upright,
And their inheritance shall be forever.

PSALM 37:18

But whoever drinks of the water that I shall give him will never thirst. But the water that I shall give him will become in him a fountain of water springing up into everlasting life.

JOHN 4:14

# PRAISE

---

This people I have formed for Myself;
>    They shall declare My praise.

ISAIAH 43:21

But you are a chosen generation, a royal priesthood, a holy nation, His own special people, that you may proclaim the praises of Him who called you out of darkness into His marvelous light.

1 PETER 2:9

Therefore by Him let us continually offer the sacrifice of praise to God, that is, the fruit of our lips, giving thanks to His name.

HEBREWS 13:15

Praise the LORD!
>    For it is good to sing praises to our God;
>    For it is pleasant, and praise is beautiful.

PSALM 147:1

I will call upon the LORD, who is worthy to be praised;
So shall I be saved from my enemies.

2 SAMUEL 22:4

I will bless the LORD at all times;
His praise shall continually be in my mouth.

PSALM 34:1

Oh, clap your hands, all you peoples!
Shout to God with the voice of triumph! . . .
Sing praises to God, sing praises!
Sing praises to our King, sing praises!
For God is the King of all the earth;
Sing praises with understanding.

PSALM 47:1, 6–7

Great is the LORD, and greatly to be praised
In the city of our God,
In His holy mountain.

PSALM 48:1

It is good to give thanks to the LORD,
And to sing praises to Your name, O Most High.

PSALM 92:1

Whoever offers praise glorifies Me;
And to him who orders his conduct aright
I will show the salvation of God.

PSALM 50:23

Because your lovingkindness is better than life,
My lips shall praise You.
Thus I will bless You while I live;
I will lift up my hands in Your name.
My soul shall be satisfied as with marrow and
fatness,
And my mouth shall praise You with joyful lips.

PSALM 63:3–5

Let my mouth be filled with Your praise
And with Your glory all the day. . . .
But I will hope continually,
And will praise You yet more and more.

PSALM 71:8, 14

For the Lord is great and greatly to be praised.

PSALM 96:4

Oh, that men would give thanks to the Lord for His
        goodness,
    And for His wonderful works to the children of
        men!

PSALM 107:8

But at midnight Paul and Silas were praying and
singing hymns to God, and the prisoners were listen-
ing to them.

ACTS 16:25

# SERVING GOD

You shall walk after the Lord your God and fear Him, and keep His commandments and obey His voice; you shall serve Him and hold fast to Him.

DEUTERONOMY 13:4

I beseech you therefore, brethren, by the mercies of God, that you present your bodies a living sacrifice, holy, acceptable to God, which is your reasonable service. And do not be conformed to this world, but be transformed by the renewing of your mind, that you may prove what is that good and acceptable and perfect will of God.

ROMANS 12:1–2

No one can serve two masters; for either he will hate the one and love the other, or else he will be loyal to the one and despise the other. You cannot serve God and mammon.

MATTHEW 6:24

Then Jesus said to him, "Away with you, Satan! For it is written, 'You shall worship the Lord your God, and Him only you shall serve.' "

MATTHEW 4:10

And now, Israel, what does the Lord your God require of you, but to fear the Lord your God, to walk in all His ways and to love Him, to serve the Lord your God with all your heart and with all your soul.

DEUTERONOMY 10:12

But take careful heed to do the commandment and the law which Moses the servant of the Lord commanded you, to love the Lord your God, to walk in all His ways, to keep His commandments, to hold fast to Him, and to serve Him with all your heart and with all your soul.

JOSHUA 22:5

Be kindly affectionate to one another with brotherly love, in honor giving preference to one another; not lagging in diligence, fervent in spirit, serving the Lord; . . . distributing to the needs of the saints, given to hospitality.

ROMANS 12:10–11, 13

As for you, my son Solomon, know the God of your father, and serve Him with a loyal heart and with a willing mind; for the LORD searches all hearts and understands all the intent of the thoughts. If you seek Him, He will be found by you; but if you forsake Him, He will cast you off forever.

1 CHRONICLES 28:9

And it shall be that if you earnestly obey My commandments which I command you today, to love the LORD your God and serve Him with all your heart and with all your soul, then I will give you the rain for your land in its season, the early rain and the latter rain, that you may gather in your grain, your new wine, and your oil. And I will send grass in your fields for your livestock, that you may eat and be filled.

DEUTERONOMY 11:13–15

But now we have been delivered from the law, having died to what we were held by, so that we should serve in the newness of the Spirit and not in the oldness of the letter.

ROMANS 7:6

And if it seems evil to you to serve the LORD, choose for yourselves this day whom you will serve, whether the gods which your fathers served that were on the other side of the River, or the gods of the Amorites, in whose land you dwell. But as for me and my house, we will serve the LORD.

JOSHUA 24:15

Then Samuel said to the people, "Do not fear. You have done all this wickedness; yet do not turn aside from following the LORD, but serve the LORD with all your heart. And do not turn aside; for then you would go after empty things which cannot profit or deliver, for they are nothing. For the LORD will not forsake His people, for His great name's sake, because it has pleased the LORD to make you His people."

1 SAMUEL 12:20–22

So you shall serve the LORD your God, and He will bless your bread and your water. And I will take sickness away from the midst of you. No one shall suffer miscarriage or be barren in your land; I will fulfill the number of your days.

EXODUS 23:25–26

Make a joyful shout to the LORD, all you lands!
    Serve the LORD with gladness;
    Come before His presence with singing. . . .
    Enter into His gates with thanksgiving,
    And into His courts with praise.
    Be thankful to Him, and bless His name.

PSALM 100:1–2, 4

# OBEDIENCE

Behold, I set before you today a blessing and a curse: the blessing, if you obey the commandments of the LORD your God which I command you today; and the curse, if you do not obey the commandments of the LORD your God, but turn aside from the way which I command you today, to go after other gods which you have not known.

DEUTERONOMY 11:26–28

So Samuel said:

"Has the LORD as great delight in burnt offerings
    and sacrifices,
As in obeying the voice of the LORD?
Behold, to obey is better than sacrifice,
And to heed than the fat of rams."

1 SAMUEL 15:22

But Peter and the other apostles answered and said: "We ought to obey God rather than men."

ACTS 5:29

Oh, that you had heeded My commandments!
    Then your peace would have been like a river,
    And your righteousness like the waves of the sea.

ISAIAH 48:18

But this is what I commanded them, saying, "Obey My voice, and I will be your God, and you shall be My people. And walk in all the ways that I have commanded you, that it may be well with you."

JEREMIAH 7:23

Now by this we know that we know Him, if we keep His commandments. He who says, "I know Him," and does not keep His commandments, is a liar, and the truth is not in him. But whoever keeps His word, truly the love of God is perfected in him. By this we know that we are in Him. He who says he abides in Him ought himself also to walk just as He walked.

1 JOHN 2:3–6

So if you walk in My ways, to keep My statutes and My commandments, as your father David walked, then I will lengthen your days.

1 KINGS 3:14

Teach me to do Your will,
> For You are my God;
> Your Spirit is good.
> Lead me in the land of uprightness.

PSALM 143:10

And Moses called all Israel, and said to them: "Hear, O Israel, the statutes and judgments which I speak in your hearing today, that you may learn them and be careful to observe them. . . .

"Therefore you shall be careful to do as the LORD your God has commanded you; you shall not turn aside to the right hand or to the left. You shall walk in all the ways which the LORD your God has commanded you, that you may live and that it may be well with you, and that you may prolong your days in the land which you shall possess."

DEUTERONOMY 5:1, 32–33

If you love Me, keep My commandment. . . .

He who has My commandments and keeps them, it is he who loves Me. And he who loves Me will be loved by My Father, and I will love him and manifest Myself to him.

JOHN 14:15, 21

Bondservants, obey in all things your masters according to the flesh, not with eyeservice, as men-pleasers, but in sincerity of heart, fearing God. And whatever you do, do it heartily, as to the Lord and not to men, knowing that from the Lord you will receive the reward of the inheritance; for you serve the Lord Christ.

COLOSSIANS 3:22–24

Children, obey your parents in all things, for this is well pleasing to the Lord.

Fathers, do not provoke your children, lest they become discouraged.

Bondservants, obey in all things your masters according to the flesh, not with eyeservice, as men-pleasers, but in sincerity of heart, fearing God. And whatever you do, do it heartily, as to the Lord and not to men, knowing that from the Lord you will receive the reward of the inheritance; for you serve the Lord Christ.

COLOSSIANS 3:20–24

Children, obey your parents in the Lord, for this is right.

EPHESIANS 6:1

Therefore submit yourselves to every ordinance of man for the Lord's sake, whether to the king as supreme, or to governors, as to those who are sent by him for the punishment of evildoers and for the praise of those who do good. For this is the will of God, that by doing good you may put to silence the ignorance of foolish men—as free, yet not using liberty as a cloak for vice, but as bondservants of God. Honor all people. Love the brotherhood. Fear God. Honor the king.

Servants, be submissive to your masters with all fear, not only to the good and gentle, but also to the harsh. For this is commendable, if because of conscience toward God one endures grief, suffering wrongfully. For what credit is it if, when you are beaten for your faults, you take it patiently? But when you do good and suffer, if you take it patiently, this is commendable before God.

1 PETER 2:13–20

WHAT THE BIBLE HAS TO SAY ABOUT . . .

# THE CARNAL MIND

For to be carnally minded is death, but to be spiritually minded is life and peace. Because the carnal mind is enmity against God; for it is not subject to the law of God, nor indeed can be. So then, those who are in the flesh cannot please God.

ROMANS 8:6–8

For he who sows to his flesh will of the flesh reap corruption, but he who sows to the Spirit will of the Spirit reap everlasting life.

GALATIANS 6:8

Adulterers and adulteresses! Do you not know that friendship with the world is enmity with God? Whoever therefore wants to be a friend of the world makes himself an enemy of God.

JAMES 4:4

But she who lives in pleasure is dead while she lives.

1 TIMOTHY 5:6

There is a way that seems right to a man,
But its end is the way of death.

PROVERBS 14:12

For many walk, of whom I have told you often, and now tell you even weeping, that they are the enemies of the cross of Christ: whose end is destruction, whose god is their belly, and whose glory is in their shame—who set their mind on earthly things.

PHILIPPIANS 3:18–19

No one engaged in warfare entangles himself with the affairs of this life, that he may please him who enlisted him as a soldier. . . .

Flee also youthful lusts; but pursue righteousness, faith, love, peace with those who call on the Lord out of a pure heart.

2 TIMOTHY 2:4, 22

You will keep him in perfect peace,
Whose mind is stayed on You,
Because he trusts in You.

ISAIAH 26:3

For men will be lovers of themselves, lovers of money, boasters, proud, blasphemers, disobedient to parents, unthankful, unholy, unloving, unforgiving, slanderers, without self-control, brutal, despisers of good, traitors, headstrong, haughty, lovers of pleasure rather than lovers of God, having a form of godliness but denying its power. And from such people turn away! For of this sort are those who creep into households and make captives of gullible women loaded down with sins, led away by various lusts, always learning and never able to come to the knowledge of the truth.

2 TIMOTHY 3:2–7

Beloved, I beg you as sojourners and pilgrims, abstain from fleshly lusts which war against the soul.

1 PETER 2:11

Set your mind on things above, not on things on the earth. . . .

Therefore put to death your members which are on the earth: fornication, uncleanness, passion, evil desire, and covetousness, which is idolatry.

COLOSSIANS 3:2, 5

Do not love the world or the things in the world. If anyone loves the world, the love of the Father is not in him. For all that is in the world—the lust of the flesh, the lust of the eyes, and the pride of life—is not of the Father but is of the world. And the world is passing away, and the lust of it; but he who does the will of God abides forever.

1 JOHN 2:15–17

I beseech you therefore, brethren, by the mercies of God, that you present your bodies a living sacrifice, holy, acceptable to God, which is your reasonable service. And do not be conformed to this world, but be transformed by the renewing of your mind, that you may prove what is that good and acceptable and perfect will of God.

ROMANS 12:1–2

Let this mind be in you which was also in Christ Jesus.

PHILIPPIANS 2:5

Finally, brethren, whatever things are true, whatever things are noble, whatever things are just, whatever things are pure, whatever things are lovely, whatever things are of good report, if there is any virtue and if there is anything praiseworthy—meditate on these things.

PHILIPPIANS 4:8

WHAT THE BIBLE HAS TO SAY ABOUT . . .

# THE GRACE OF GOD

And with great power the apostles gave witness to the resurrection of the Lord Jesus. And great grace was upon them all.

ACTS 4:33

And so find favor and high esteem
    In the sight of God and man.

PROVERBS 3:4

For the LORD God is a sun and shield;
    The LORD will give grace and glory;
    No good thing will He withhold
    From those who walk uprightly.

PSALM 84:11

So the LORD said to Moses, "I will also do this thing that you have spoken; for you have found grace in My sight, and I know you by name."

EXODUS 33:17

You have granted me life and favor,
And Your care has preserved my spirit.

JOB 10:12

For You, O LORD, will bless the righteous;
With favor You will surround him as with a shield.

PSALM 5:12

LORD, by Your favor You have made my mountain
stand strong;
You hid Your face, and I was troubled.

PSALM 30:7

The LORD has been mindful of us;
He will bless us;
He will bless the house of Israel;
He will bless the house of Aaron.
He will bless those who fear the LORD,
Both small and great.

PSALM 115:12–13

For whoever finds me finds life,
And obtains favor from the LORD.

PROVERBS 8:35

Blessings are on the head of the righteous,
But violence covers the mouth of the wicked. . . .
The blessing of the LORD makes one rich,
And He adds no sorrow with it. . . .
The fear of the wicked will come upon him,
And the desire of the righteous will be granted.

PROVERBS 10:6, 22, 24

Fools mock at sin,
But among the upright there is favor.

PROVERBS 14:9

The sons of foreigners shall build up your walls,
And their kings shall minister to you;
For in My wrath I struck you,
But in My favor I have had mercy on you.

ISAIAH 60:10

For all things are for your sakes, that grace, having spread through the many, may cause thanksgiving to abound to the glory of God.

2 CORINTHIANS 4:15

To the praise of the glory of His grace, by which He made us accepted in the Beloved.

EPHESIANS 1:6

Let us therefore come boldly to the throne of grace, that we may obtain mercy and find grace to help in time of need.

HEBREWS 4:16

# THE HOLY SPIRIT

Or do you not know that your body is the temple of the Holy Spirit who is in you, whom you have from God, and you are not your own?

1 CORINTHIANS 6:19

Now hope does not disappoint, because the love of God has been poured out in our hearts by the Holy Spirit who was given to us.

ROMANS 5:5

And I will pray the Father, and He will give you another Helper, that He may abide with you forever—the Spirit of truth, whom the world cannot receive, because it neither sees Him nor knows Him; but you know Him, for He dwells with you and will be in you.

JOHN 14:16–17

And do not be drunk with wine, in which is dissipation; but be filled with the Spirit.

EPHESIANS 5:18

Nevertheless I tell you the truth. It is to your advantage that I go away; for if I do not go away, the Helper will not come to you; but if I depart, I will send Him to you. . . .

However, when He, the Spirit of truth, has come, He will guide you into all truth; for He will not speak on His own authority, but whatever He hears He will speak; and He will tell you things to come.

JOHN 16:7, 13

I indeed baptize you with water unto repentance, but He who is coming after me is mightier than I, whose sandals I am not worthy to carry. He will baptize you with the Holy Spirit and fire.

MATTHEW 3:11

He who believes in Me, as the Scripture has said, out of his heart will flow rivers of living water. But this He spoke concerning the Spirit, whom those believing in Him would receive; for the Holy Spirit was not yet given, because Jesus was not yet glorified.

JOHN 7:38–39

If you then, being evil, know how to give good gifts to your children, how much more will your heavenly Father give the Holy Spirit to those who ask Him!

LUKE 11:13

And it shall come to pass afterward
    That I will pour out My spirit on all flesh;
    Your sons and your daughters shall prophesy,
    Your old men shall dream dreams,
    Your young men shall see visions.

JOEL 2:28

And being assembled together with them, He commanded them not to depart from Jerusalem, but to wait for the promise of the Father, "which," He said, "you have heard from Me; for John truly baptized with water, but you shall be baptized with the Holy Spirit not many days from now. . . .

"But you shall receive power when the Holy Spirit has come upon you; and you shall be witnesses to Me in Jerusalem, and in all Judea and Samaria, and to the end of the earth."

ACTS 1:4–5, 8

He said to them, "Did you receive the Holy Spirit when you believed?"

So they said to him, "We have not so much as heard whether there is a Holy Spirit."

And he said to them, "Into what then were you baptized?"

So they said, "Into John's baptism."

Then Paul said, "John indeed baptized with a baptism of repentance, saying to the people that they should believe on him who would come after him, that is, on Christ Jesus."

When they heard this, they were baptized in the name of the Lord Jesus. And when Paul had laid hands on them, the Holy Spirit came upon them, and they spoke with tongues and prophesied.

ACTS 19:2–6

Then Peter said to them, "Repent, and let every one of you be baptized in the name of Jesus Christ for the remission of sins; and you shall receive the gift of the Holy Spirit."

ACTS 2:38

And when they had prayed, the place where they were assembled together was shaken; and they were all filled with the Holy Spirit, and they spoke the word of God with boldness.

ACTS 4:31

Now when the apostles who were at Jerusalem heard that Samaria had received the word of God, they sent Peter and John to them, who, when they had come down, prayed for them that they might receive the Holy Spirit. For as yet He had fallen upon none of them. They had only been baptized in the name of the Lord Jesus. Then they laid hands on them, and they received the Holy Spirit.

ACTS 8:14–17

While Peter was still speaking these words, the Holy Spirit fell upon all those who heard the word. And those of the circumcision who believed were astonished, as many as came with Peter, because the gift of the Holy Spirit had been poured out on the Gentiles also. For they heard them speak with tongues and magnify God.

ACTS 10:44–46

And they were all filled with the Holy Spirit and began to speak with other tongues, as the Spirit gave them utterance.

ACTS 2:4

WHAT THE BIBLE HAS TO SAY ABOUT . . .

# GOD'S FAITHFULNESS

You have dealt well with Your servant,
    O Lord, according to Your word.

PSALM 119:65

He who calls you is faithful, who also will do it.

1 THESSALONIANS 5:24

"For this is like the waters of Noah to Me;
    For as I have sworn
    That the waters of Noah would no longer cover
        the earth,
    So have I sworn
    That I would not be angry with you, nor rebuke
        you.
    For the mountains shall depart
    And the hills be removed,
    But My kindness shall not depart from you,
    Nor shall My covenant of peace be removed,"
    Says the Lord, who has mercy on you.

ISAIAH 54:9–10

The rainbow shall be in the cloud, and I will look on it to remember the everlasting covenant between God and every living creature of all flesh that is on the earth.

GENESIS 9:16

Behold, I am with you and will keep you wherever you go, and will bring you back to this land; for I will not leave you until I have done what I have spoken to you.

GENESIS 28:15

But because the Lord loves you, and because He would keep the oath which He swore to your fathers, the Lord has brought you out with a mighty hand, and redeemed you from the house of bondage, from the hand of Pharaoh king of Egypt.

Therefore know that the Lord your God, He is God, the faithful God who keeps covenant and mercy for a thousand generations with those who love Him and keep His commandments.

DEUTERONOMY 7:8–9

Behold, this day I am going the way of all the earth. And you know in all your hearts and in all your souls that not one thing has failed of all the good things which the LORD your God spoke concerning you. All have come to pass for you; not one word of them has failed.

JOSHUA 23:14

Blessed be the LORD, who has given rest to His people Israel, according to all that He promised. There has not failed one word of all His good promise, which He promised through His servant Moses.

1 KINGS 8:56

Your mercy, O LORD, is in the heavens;
    Your faithfulness reaches to the clouds.

PSALM 36:5

He will not allow your foot to be moved;
    He who keeps you will not slumber.
    Behold, He who keeps Israel
    Shall neither slumber nor sleep.

PSALM 121:3–4

I will sing of the mercies of the Lord forever;
 With my mouth will I make known Your
  faithfulness to all generations.
 For I have said, "Mercy shall be built up forever;
 Your faithfulness You shall establish in the very
  heavens. . . .
"Nevertheless My lovingkindness I will not utterly
  take from him,
 Nor allow My faithfulness to fail.
 My covenant I will not break,
 Nor alter the word that has gone out of My lips."

PSALM 89:1–2, 33–34

God is faithful, by whom you were called into the fellowship of His Son, Jesus Christ our Lord.

1 CORINTHIANS 1:9

No temptation has overtaken you except such as is common to man; but God is faithful, who will not allow you to be tempted beyond what you are able, but with the temptation will also make the way of escape, that you may be able to bear it.

1 CORINTHIANS 10:13

The Lord is not slack concerning His promise, as some count slackness, but is longsuffering toward us, not willing that any should perish but that all should come to repentance.

2 PETER 3:9

If we are faithless,
He remains faithful;
He cannot deny himself. . . .

Nevertheless the solid foundation of God stands, having this seal: "The Lord knows those who are His," and, "Let everyone who names the name of Christ depart from iniquity."

2 TIMOTHY 2:13, 19

WHAT THE BIBLE HAS TO SAY ABOUT . . .

# THE CHURCH

---

That in the dispensation of the fullness of the times He might gather together in one all things in Christ, both which are in heaven and which are on earth—in Him. . . .

And He put all things under His feet, and gave Him to be head over all things to the church, which is His body, the fullness of Him who fills all in all.

EPHESIANS 1:10, 22–23

He has delivered us from the power of darkness and conveyed us into the kingdom of the Son of His love. . . .

And He is the head of the body, the church, who is the beginning, the firstborn from the dead, that in all things He may have the preeminence.

COLOSSIANS 1:13, 18

Behold, how good and how pleasant it is
For brethren to dwell together in unity!

PSALM 133:1

Having been built on the foundation of the apostles and prophets, Jesus Christ Himself being the chief cornerstone, in whom the whole building, being fitted together, grows into a holy temple in the Lord, In whom you also are being built together for a dwelling place of God in the Spirit.

EPHESIANS 2:20–22

For the husband is head of the wife, as also Christ is head of the church; and He is the Savior of the body. Therefore, just as the church is subject to Christ, so let the wives be to their own husbands in everything.

Husbands, love your wives, just as Christ also loved the church and gave Himself for her, that He might sanctify and cleanse her with the washing of water by the word, that He might present her to Himself a glorious church, not having spot or wrinkle or any such thing, but that she should be holy and without blemish. . . .

For no one ever hated his own flesh, but nourishes and cherishes it, just as the Lord does the church.

EPHESIANS 5:23–27, 29

Remember those who rule over you, who have spoken the word of God to you, whose faith follow, considering the outcome of their conduct. . . .

Obey those who rule over you, and be submissive, for they watch out for your souls, as those who must give account. Let them do so with joy and not with grief, for that would be unprofitable for you.

HEBREWS 13:7, 17

For as we have many members in one body, but all the members do not have the same function, so we, being many, are one body in Christ, and individually members of one another.

ROMANS 12:4–5

And He Himself gave some to be apostles, some prophets, some evangelists, and some pastors and teachers, for the equipping of the saints for the work of ministry, for the edifying of the body of Christ.

EPHESIANS 4:11–12

# STEWARDSHIP

But lay up for yourselves treasures in heaven, where neither moth nor rust destroys and where thieves do not break in and steal. For where your treasure is, there your heart will be also.

MATTHEW 6:20–21

Give, and it will be given to you: good measure, pressed down, shaken together, and running over will be put into your bosom. For with the same measure that you use, it will be measured back to you.

LUKE 6:38

Now concerning the collection for the saints, as I have given orders to the churches of Galatia, so you must do also: On the first day of the week let each one of you lay something aside, storing up as he may prosper.

1 CORINTHIANS 16:1–2

But this I say: He who sows sparingly will also reap sparingly, and he who sows bountifully will also reap bountifully. So let each one give as he purposes in his heart, not grudgingly or of necessity; for God loves a cheerful giver. And God is able to make all grace abound toward you, that you, always having all sufficiency in all things, may have an abundance for every good work.

2 CORINTHIANS 9:6–8

And whatever you do, do it heartily, as to the Lord and not to men, knowing that from the Lord you will receive the reward of the inheritance; for you serve the Lord Christ.

COLOSSIANS 3:23–24

Beloved, I pray that you may prosper in all things and be in health, just as your soul prospers.

3 JOHN V. 2

But seek first the kingdom of God and His righteousness, and all these things shall be added to you.

MATTHEW 6:33

And everyone who has left houses or brothers or sisters or father or mother or wife or children or lands, for My name's sake, shall receive a hundredfold, and inherit eternal life.

MATTHEW 19:29

Heal the sick, cleanse the lepers, raise the dead, cast out demons. Freely you have received, freely give.

MATTHEW 10:8

Therefore keep the words of this covenant, and do them, that you may prosper in all that you do.

DEUTERONOMY 29:9

Then you will prosper, if you take care to fulfill the statutes and judgments with which the LORD charged Moses concerning Israel.

1 CHRONICLES 22:13

If they obey and serve Him,
    They shall spend their days in prosperity,
    And their years in pleasures.

JOB 36:11

There is one who scatters, yet increases more;
   And there is one who withholds more than is right,
   But it leads to poverty.
   The generous soul will be made rich,
   And he who waters will also be watered himself.

PROVERBS 11:24–25

So Jesus answered and said, "Assuredly, I say to you, there is no one who has left house or brothers or sisters or father or mother or wife or children or lands, for My sake and the gospel's, who shall not receive a hundredfold now in this time—houses and brothers and sisters and mothers and children and lands, with persecutions—and in the age to come, eternal life."

MARK 10:29–30

This Book of the Law shall not depart from your mouth, but you shall meditate in it day and night, that you may observe to do according to all that is written in it. For then you will make your way prosperous, and then you will have good success.

JOSHUA 1:8

# SATAN

Be sober, be vigilant; because your adversary the devil walks about like a roaring lion, seeking whom he may devour. Resist him, steadfast in the faith.

1 PETER 5:8–9

Therefore submit to God. Resist the devil and he will flee from you.

JAMES 4:7

But we see Jesus, who was made a little lower than the angels, for the suffering of death crowned with glory and honor, that He, by the grace of God, might taste death for everyone. . . .

Inasmuch then as the children have partaken of flesh and blood, He Himself likewise shared in the same, that through death He might destroy him who had the power of death, that is, the devil, and release those who through fear of death were all their lifetime subject to bondage.

HEBREWS 2:9, 14–15

Finally, my brethren, be strong in the Lord and in the power of His might. Put on the whole armor of God, that you may be able to stand against the wiles of the devil. For we do not wrestle against flesh and blood, but against principalities, against powers, against the rulers of the darkness of this age, against spiritual hosts of wickedness in the heavenly places. Therefore take up the whole armor of God, that you may be able to withstand in the evil day, and having done all, to stand.

Stand therefore, having girded your waist with truth, having put on the breastplate of righteousness, and having shod your feet with the preparation of the gospel of peace; above all, taking the shield of faith with which you will be able to quench all the fiery darts of the wicked one. And take the helmet of salvation, and the sword of the Spirit, which is the word of God; praying always with all prayer and supplication in the Spirit, being watchful to this end with all perseverance and supplication for all the saints.

EPHESIANS 6:10–18

And you are complete in Him, who is the head of all principality and power. . . .

Having disarmed principalities and powers, He made a public spectacle of them, triumphing over them in it.

COLOSSIANS 2:10, 15

He has delivered us from the power of darkness and conveyed us into the kingdom of the Son of His love.

COLOSSIANS 1:13

And they overcame him by the blood of the Lamb and by the word of their testimony, and they did not love their lives to the death.

REVELATION 12:11

For though we walk in the flesh, we do not war according to the flesh. For the weapons of our warfare are not carnal but mighty in God for pulling down strongholds, casting down arguments and every high thing that exalts itself against the knowledge of God, bringing every thought into captivity to the obedience of Christ.

2 CORINTHIANS 10:3–5

Beloved, do not believe every spirit, but test the spirits, whether they are of God; because many false prophets have gone out into the world. By this you know the Spirit of God: Every spirit that confesses that Jesus Christ has come in the flesh is of God, and every spirit that does not confess that Jesus Christ has come in the flesh is not of God. And this is the spirit of the Antichrist, which you have heard was coming, and is now already in the world.

You are of God, little children, and have overcome them, because He who is in you is greater than he who is in the world.

1 JOHN 4:1–4

Then the seventy returned with joy, saying, "Lord, even the demons are subject to us in Your name."

And He said to them, "I saw Satan fall like lightning from heaven. Behold, I give you the authority to trample on serpents and scorpions, and over all the power of the enemy, and nothing shall by any means hurt you."

LUKE 10:17–19

And these signs will follow those who believe: In My name they will cast out demons; they will speak with new tongues; they will take up serpents; and if they drink anything deadly, it will by no means hurt them; they will lay hands on the sick, and they will recover.

MARK 16:17–18

But if I cast out demons by the Spirit of God, surely the kingdom of God has come upon you. Or how can one enter a strong man's house and plunder his goods, unless he first binds the strong man? And then he will plunder his house.

MATTHEW 12:28–29

The name of the Lord is a strong tower;
    The righteous run to it and are safe.

PROVERBS 18:10

He who sins is of the devil, for the devil has sinned from the beginning. For this purpose the Son of God was manifested, that He might destroy the works of the devil.

1 JOHN 3:8

And the God of peace will crush Satan under your feet shortly.

The grace of our Lord Jesus Christ be with you. Amen.

ROMANS 16:20

I write to you, fathers,
> Because you have known Him who is from the beginning.

I write to you, young men,
> Because you have overcome the wicked one.

I write to you, little children,
> Because you have known the Father.

I have written to you, fathers,
> Because you have known Him who is from the beginning.

I have written to you, young men,
> Because you are strong, and the word of God abides in you,
> And you have overcome the wicked one.

1 JOHN 2:13–14

# THE RETURN OF CHRIST

And there will be signs in the sun, in the moon, and in the stars; and on the earth distress of nations, with perplexity, the sea and the waves roaring; men's hearts failing them from fear and the expectation of those things which are coming on the earth, for the powers of the heavens will be shaken. Then they will see the Son of Man coming in a cloud with power and great glory. Now when these things begin to happen, look up and lift up your heads, because your redemption draws near.

LUKE 21:25–28

Beloved, now we are children of God; and it has not yet been revealed what we shall be, but we know that when He is revealed, we shall be like Him, for we shall see Him as He is. And everyone who has this hope in Him purifies himself, just as He is pure.

1 JOHN 3:2–3

Behold, I tell you a mystery: We shall not all sleep, but we shall all be changed—in a moment, in the twinkling of an eye, at the last trumpet. For the trumpet will sound, and the dead will be raised incorruptible, and we shall be changed. For this corruptible must put on incorruption, and this mortal must put on immortality. So when this corruptible has put on incorruption, and this mortal has put on immortality, then shall be brought to pass the saying that is written: "Death is swallowed up in victory."

"O Death, where is your sting?

O Hades, where is your victory?"

The sting of death is sin, and the strength of sin is the law. But thanks be to God, who gives us the victory through our Lord Jesus Christ.

1 CORINTHIANS 15:51–57

Who also said, "Men of Galilee, why do you stand gazing up into heaven? This same Jesus, who was taken up from you into heaven, will so come in like manner as you saw Him go into heaven."

ACTS 1:11

Beloved, do not forget this one thing, that with the Lord one day is as a thousand years, and a thousand years as one day. The Lord is not slack concerning His promise, as some count slackness, but is long-suffering toward us, not willing that any should perish but that all should come to repentance.

But the day of the Lord will come as a thief in the night, in which the heavens will pass away with a great noise, and the elements will melt with fervent heat; both the earth and the works that are in it will be burned up. Therefore, since all these things will be dissolved, what manner of persons ought you to be in holy conduct and godliness, looking for and hastening the coming of the day of God, because of which the heavens will be dissolved, being on fire, and the elements will melt with fervent heat? Nevertheless we, according to His promise, look for new heavens and a new earth in which righteousness dwells.

2 PETER 3:8–13

Jesus answered and said to them: "Take heed that no one deceives you. For many will come in my name, saying, 'I am the Christ,' and will deceive many. And you will hear of wars and rumors of wars. See that you are not troubled; for all these things must come to pass, but the end is not yet. For nation will rise against nation, and kingdom against kingdom. And there will be famines, pestilences, and earthquakes in various places. All these are the beginning of sorrows.

"Then they will deliver you up to tribulation and kill you, and you will be hated by all nations for my name's sake. And then many will be offended, will betray one another, and will hate one another. Then many false prophets will rise up and deceive many. And because lawlessness will abound, the love of many will grow cold. But he who endures to the end shall be saved. And this gospel of the kingdom will be preached in all the world as a witness to all the nations, and then the end will come."

MATTHEW 24:4–14

For as the lightning comes from the east and flashes to the west, so also will the coming of the Son of Man be. . . .

Immediately after the tribulation of those days the sun will be darkened, and the moon will not give its light; the stars will fall from heaven, and the powers of the heavens will be shaken. Then the sign of the Son of Man will appear in heaven, and then all the tribes of the earth will mourn, and they will see the Son of Man coming on the clouds of heaven with power and great glory. And He will send His angels with a great sound of a trumpet, and they will gather together His elect from the four winds, from one end of heaven to the other.

MATTHEW 24:27, 29–31

Let not your heart be troubled; you believe in God, believe also in Me. In My Father's house are many mansions; if it were not so, I would have told you. I go to prepare a place for you. And if I go and prepare a place for you, I will come again and receive you to Myself; that where I am, there you may be also. And where I go you know, and the way you know.

JOHN 14:1–4

But of that day and hour no one knows, not even the angels of heaven, but My Father only. But as the days of Noah were, so also will the coming of the Son of Man be. For as in the days before the flood, they were eating and drinking, marrying and giving in marriage, until the day that Noah entered the ark, and did not know until the flood came and took them all away, so also will the coming of the Son of Man be. Then two men will be in the field: one will be taken and the other left. Two women will be grinding at the mill: one will be taken and the other left. Watch therefore, for you do not know what hour your Lord is coming. But know this, that if the master of the house had known what hour the thief would come, he would have watched and not allowed his house to be broken into. Therefore you also be ready, for the Son of Man is coming at an hour you do not expect.

MATTHEW 24:36–44

Assuredly, I say to you, this generation will by no means pass away till all these things take place.

MATTHEW 24:34

But know this, that in the last days perilous times will come: For men will be lovers of themselves, lovers of money, boasters, proud, blasphemers, disobedient to parents, unthankful, unholy, unloving, unforgiving, slanderers, without self-control, brutal, despisers of good, traitors, headstrong, haughty, lovers of pleasure rather than lovers of God, having a form of godliness but denying its power. And from such people turn away!

2 TIMOTHY 3:1–5

# THE UNSAVED

For all have sinned and fall short of the glory of God.

ROMANS 3:23

Therefore, just as through one man sin entered the world, and death through sin, and thus death spread to all men, because all sinned.

ROMANS 5:12

For the wrath of God is revealed from heaven against all ungodliness and unrighteousness of men, who suppress the truth in unrighteousness, because what may be known of God is manifest in them, for God has shown it to them. For since the creation of the world His invisible attributes are clearly seen, being understood by the things that are made, even His eternal power and Godhead, so that they are without excuse.

ROMANS 1:18–20

For the wages of sin is death, but the gift of God is eternal life in Christ Jesus our Lord.

ROMANS 6:23

The Lord is not slack concerning His promise, as some count slackness, but is longsuffering toward us, not willing that any should perish but that all should come to repentance.

2 PETER 3:9

But God demonstrates His own love toward us, in that while we were still sinners, Christ died for us.

ROMANS 5:8

For God so loved the world that He gave His only begotten Son, that whoever believes in Him should not perish but have everlasting life.

JOHN 3:16

For God did not send His Son into the world to condemn the world, but that the world through Him might be saved.

JOHN 3:17

For the Son of Man has come to seek and to save that which was lost.

LUKE 19:10

Jesus answered and said to him, "Most assuredly, I say to you, unless one is born again, he cannot see the kingdom of God."

JOHN 3:3

And He said to them, "Go into all the world and preach the gospel to every creature. He who believes and is baptized will be saved; but he who does not believe will be condemned."

MARK 16:15–16

The Spirit of the Lord is upon Me,
    Because He has anointed Me
    To preach the gospel to the poor;
    He has sent Me to heal the brokenhearted,
    To proclaim liberty to the captives
    And recovery of sight to the blind,
    To set at liberty those who are oppressed;
    To proclaim the acceptable year of the Lord.

LUKE 4:18–19

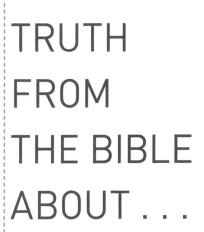

TRUTH
FROM
THE BIBLE
ABOUT . . .

# FORGIVING OTHERS

For if you forgive men their trespasses, your heavenly Father will also forgive you. But if you do not forgive men their trespasses, neither will your Father forgive your trespasses.

MATTHEW 6:14–15

Then Peter came to Him and said, "Lord, how often shall my brother sin against me, and I forgive him? Up to seven times?"

Jesus said to him, "I do not say to you, up to seven times, but up to seventy times seven."

MATTHEW 18:21–22

Take heed to yourselves. If your brother sins against you, rebuke him; and if he repents, forgive him.

LUKE 17:3

Do not be overcome by evil, but overcome evil with good.

ROMANS 12:21

For we know Him who said, "Vengeance is Mine, I will repay," says the Lord. And again, "The Lord will judge His people."

HEBREWS 10:30

And whenever you stand praying, if you have anything against anyone, forgive him, that your Father in heaven may also forgive you your trespasses.

MARK 11:25

Bearing with one another, and forgiving one another, if anyone has a complaint against another; even as Christ forgave you, so you also must do.

COLOSSIANS 3:13

Brethren, I do not count myself to have apprehended; but one thing I do, forgetting those things which are behind and reaching forward to those things which are ahead, I press toward the goal for the prize of the upward call of God in Christ Jesus.

PHILIPPIANS 3:13–14

Do not remember the former things,
    Nor consider the things of old.
    Behold, I will do a new thing,
    Now it shall spring forth;
    Shall you not know it?
    I will even make a road in the wilderness
    And rivers in the desert.

ISAIAH 43:18–19

For this is commendable, if because of conscience toward God one endures grief, suffering wrongfully. For what credit is it if, when you are beaten for your faults, you take it patiently? But when you do good and suffer, if you take it patiently, this is commendable before God. For to this you were called, because Christ also suffered for us, leaving us an example, that you should follow His steps:

    "Who committed no sin,
    Nor was deceit found in his mouth."

who, when He was reviled, did not revile in return; when He suffered, He did not threaten, but committed Himself to Him who judges righteously.

1 PETER 2:19–23

Not returning evil for evil or reviling for reviling, but on the contrary blessing, knowing that you were called to this, that you may inherit a blessing. For

"He who would love life
And see good days,
Let him refrain his tongue from evil,
And his lips from speaking deceit."

1 PETER 3:9–10

Let all bitterness, wrath, anger, clamor, and evil speaking be put away from you, with all malice. And be kind to one another, tenderhearted, forgiving one another, even as God in Christ forgave you.

EPHESIANS 4:31–32

Blessed are those who are persecuted for
righteousness' sake,
For theirs is the kingdom of heaven.
Blessed are you when they revile and persecute you, and say all kinds of evil against you falsely for My sake. Rejoice and be exceedingly glad, for great is your reward in heaven, for so they persecuted the prophets who were before you.

MATTHEW 5:10–12

# CHRISTIAN FELLOWSHIP

That which we have seen and heard we declare to you, that you also may have fellowship with us; and truly our fellowship is with the Father and with His Son Jesus Christ. . . .

But if we walk in the light as He is in the light, we have fellowship with one another, and the blood of Jesus Christ His Son cleanses us from all sin.

1 JOHN 1:3, 7

And walk in love, as Christ also has loved us and given Himself for us, an offering and a sacrifice to God for a sweet-smelling aroma. . . .

Speaking to one another in psalms and hymns and spiritual songs, singing and making melody in your heart to the Lord. . . .

For we are members of His body, of His flesh and of His bones.

EPHESIANS 5:2, 19, 30

Let the word of Christ dwell in you richly in all wisdom, teaching and admonishing one another in psalms and hymns and spiritual songs, singing with grace in your hearts to the Lord.

COLOSSIANS 3:16

That their hearts may be encouraged, being knit together in love, and attaining to all riches of the full assurance of understanding, to the knowledge of the mystery of God, both of the Father and of Christ.

COLOSSIANS 2:2

Now, therefore, you are no longer strangers and foreigners, but fellow citizens with the saints and members of the household of God, having been built on the foundation of the apostles and prophets, Jesus Christ Himself being the chief cornerstone, in whom the whole building, being fitted together, grows into a holy temple in the Lord, in whom you also are being built together for a dwelling place of God in the Spirit.

EPHESIANS 2:19–22

Then those who feared the LORD spoke to one
    another,
  And the LORD listened and heard them;
  So a book of remembrance was written before Him
  For those who fear the LORD
  And who meditate on His name.

MALACHI 3:16

Now behold, two of them were traveling that same day to a village called Emmaus, which was seven miles from Jerusalem. And they talked together of all these things which had happened. So it was, while they conversed and reasoned, that Jesus Himself drew near and went with them.

LUKE 24:13–15

Now may the God of patience and comfort grant you to be like-minded toward one another, according to Christ Jesus, that you may with one mind and one mouth glorify the God and Father of our Lord Jesus Christ.

Therefore receive one another, just as Christ also received us, to the glory of God.

ROMANS 15:5–7

We took sweet counsel together,
    And walked to the house of God in the throng.

PSALM 55:14

Now I plead with you, brethren, by the name of our Lord Jesus Christ, that you all speak the same thing, and that there be no divisions among you, but that you be perfectly joined together in the same mind and in the same judgment.

1 CORINTHIANS 1:10

Bear one another's burdens, and so fulfill the law of Christ. . . .

Therefore, as we have opportunity, let us do good to all, especially to those who are of the household of faith.

GALATIANS 6:2, 10

Therefore if there is any consolation in Christ, if any comfort of love, if any fellowship of the Spirit, if any affection and mercy, fulfill my joy by being like-minded, having the same love, being of one accord, of one mind.

PHILIPPIANS 2:1–2

TRUTH FROM THE BIBLE ABOUT . . .

# YOUR RESPONSIBILITY

And He said to them, "Go into all the world and preach the gospel to every creature."

MARK 16:15

But you shall receive power when the Holy Spirit has come upon you; and you shall be witnesses to Me in Jerusalem, and in all Judea and Samaria, and to the end of the earth.

ACTS 1:8

By this we know love, because He laid down His life for us. And we also ought to lay down our lives for the brethren. But whoever has this world's goods, and sees his brother in need, and shuts up his heart from him, how does the love of God abide in him?

My little children, let us not love in word or in tongue, but in deed and in truth.

1 JOHN 3:16–18

You are the salt of the earth; but if the salt loses its flavor, how shall it be seasoned? It is then good for nothing but to be thrown out and trampled underfoot by men.

You are the light of the world. A city that is set on a hill cannot be hidden. Nor do they light a lamp and put it under a basket, but on a lampstand, and it gives light to all who are in the house. Let your light so shine before men, that they may see your good works and glorify your Father in heaven.

MATTHEW 5:13–16

And whoever gives one of these little ones only a cup of cold water in the name of a disciple, assuredly, I say to you, he shall by no means lose his reward.

MATTHEW 10:42

So the people asked him, saying, "What shall we do then?"

He answered and said to them, "He who has two tunics, let him give to him who has none; and he who has food, let him do likewise."

LUKE 3:10–11

For God is not unjust to forget your work and labor of love which you have shown toward His name, in that you have ministered to the saints, and do minister.

HEBREWS 6:10

For I was hungry and you gave Me food; I was thirsty and you gave Me drink; I was a stranger and you took Me in; I was naked and you clothed Me; I was sick and you visited Me; I was in prison and you came to Me.

Then the righteous will answer Him, saying, "Lord, when did we see You hungry and feed You, or thirsty and give You drink? When did we see You a stranger and take You in, or naked and clothe You? Or when did we see You sick, or in prison, and come to You?" And the King will answer and say to them, "Assuredly, I say to you, inasmuch as you did it to one of the least of these My brethren, you did it to Me."

MATTHEW 25:35–40

Pure and undefiled religion before God and the Father is this: to visit orphans and widows in their trouble, and to keep oneself unspotted from the world.

JAMES 1:27

If a brother or sister is naked and destitute of daily food, and one of you says to them, "Depart in peace, be warmed and filled," but you do not give them the things which are needed for the body, what does it profit? Thus also faith by itself, if it does not have works, is dead.

JAMES 2:15–17

And these words which I command you today shall be in your heart. You shall teach them diligently to your children, and shall talk of them when you sit in your house, when you walk by the way, when you lie down, and when you rise up. You shall bind them as a sign on your hand, and they shall be as front-lets between your eyes. You shall write them on the doorposts of your house and on your gates.

DEUTERONOMY 6:6–9

But if anyone does not provide for his own, and especially for those of his household, he has denied the faith and is worse than an unbeliever.

1 TIMOTHY 5:8

TRUTH FROM THE BIBLE ABOUT . . .

# SPEAKING GOD'S WORD

For assuredly, I say to you, whoever says to this mountain, "Be removed and be cast into the sea," and does not doubt in his heart, but believes that those things he says will be done, he will have whatever he says.

MARK 11:23

So the Lord said, "If you have faith as a mustard seed, you can say to this mulberry tree, 'Be pulled up by the roots and be planted in the sea,' and it would obey you."

LUKE 17:6

For I have not spoken on My own authority; but the Father who sent Me gave Me a command, what I should say and what I should speak. And I know that His command is everlasting life. Therefore, whatever I speak, just as the Father has told Me, so I speak.

JOHN 12:49–50

Then He arose and rebuked the wind, and said to the sea, "Peace, be still!" And the wind ceased and there was a great calm.

MARK 4:39

By faith we understand that the worlds were framed by the word of God, so that the things which are seen were not made of things which are visible.

HEBREWS 11:3

I will raise up for them a Prophet like you from among their brethren, and will put My words in His mouth, and He shall speak to them all that I command Him.

DEUTERONOMY 18:18

Bless the LORD, you His angels,
    Who excel in strength, who do His word,
    Heeding the voice of His word.

PSALM 103:20

Beat your plowshares into swords
    And your pruning hooks into spears;
    Let the weak say, "I am strong."

JOEL 3:10

For out of the abundance of the heart the mouth speaks. . . . But I say to you that for every idle word men may speak, they will give account of it in the day of judgment. For by your words you will be justified, and by your words you will be condemned.

MATTHEW 12:34, 36–37

If anyone among you thinks he is religious, and does not bridle his tongue but deceives his own heart, this one's religion is useless.

JAMES 1:26

But the righteousness of faith speaks in this way. . . . But what does it say? "The word is near you, in your mouth and in your heart" (that is, the word of faith which we preach): that if you confess with your mouth the Lord Jesus and believe in your heart that God has raised Him from the dead, you will be saved. For with the heart one believes unto righteousness, and with the mouth confession is made unto salvation.

ROMANS 10:6, 8–10

Let us hold fast the confession of our hope without wavering, for He who promised is faithful.

HEBREWS 10:23

And since we have the same spirit of faith, according to what is written, "I believed and therefore I spoke," we also believe and therefore speak.

2 CORINTHIANS 4:13

A man shall eat well by the fruit of his mouth,
But the soul of the unfaithful feeds on violence.
He who guards his mouth preserves his life,
But he who opens wide his lips shall have
destruction.

PROVERBS 13:2–3

There is one who speaks like the piercings of a
sword,
But the tongue of the wise promotes health.

PROVERBS 12:18

# FINDING THE WILL OF GOD

If any of you lacks wisdom, let him ask of God, who gives to all liberally and without reproach, and it will be given to him.

JAMES 1:5

I will instruct you and teach you in the way you
        should go;
    I will guide you with My eye.

PSALM 32:8

Your word is a lamp to my feet
    And a light to my path.

PSALM 119:105

This Book of the Law shall not depart from your mouth, but you shall meditate in it day and night, that you may observe to do according to all that is written in it. For then you will make your way prosperous, and then you will have good success.

JOSHUA 1:8

When you roam, they will lead you;
  When you sleep, they will keep you;
  And when you awake, they will speak with you.
  For the commandment is a lamp,
  And the law a light;
  Reproofs of instruction are the way of life.

PROVERBS 6:22–23

Your ears shall hear a word behind you, saying,
  "This is the way, walk in it,"
  Whenever you turn to the right hand
  Or whenever you turn to the left.

ISAIAH 30:21

However, when he, the Spirit of truth, has come, He will guide you into all truth; for He will not speak on His own authority, but whatever He hears He will speak; and He will tell you things to come.

JOHN 16:13

For You are my rock and my fortress;
  Therefore, for Your name's sake,
  Lead me and guide me.

PSALM 31:3

For this is God,
Our God forever and ever;
He will be our guide
Even to death.

PSALM 48:14

The steps of a good man are ordered by the LORD,
And He delights in his way.

PSALM 37:23

Trust in the LORD with all your heart,
And lean not on your own understanding;
In all your ways acknowledge Him,
And He shall direct your paths.

PROVERBS 3:5–6

Thus says the LORD, your Redeemer,
The Holy One of Israel:
"I am the LORD your God,
Who teaches you to profit,
Who leads you by the way you should go."

ISAIAH 48:17

# ANSWERED PRAYER

It shall come to pass
    That before they call, I will answer;
    And while they are still speaking, I will hear.

ISAIAH 65:24

Ask, and it will be given to you; seek, and you will find; knock, and it will be opened to you. For everyone who asks receives, and he who seeks finds, and to him who knocks it will be opened.

MATTHEW 7:7–8

And whatever things you ask in prayer, believing, you will receive.

MATTHEW 21:22

The LORD is near to all who call upon Him,
    To all who call upon Him in truth.
    He will fulfill the desire of those who fear Him;
    He also will hear their cry and save them.

PSALM 145:18–19

Again I say to you that if two of you agree on earth concerning anything that they ask, it will be done for them by My Father in heaven. For where two or three are gathered together in My name, I am there in the midst of them.

MATTHEW 18:19–20

And whatever you ask in My name, that I will do, that the Father may be glorified in the Son.

JOHN 14:13

Therefore I say to you, whatever things you ask when you pray, believe that you receive them, and you will have them.

MARK 11:24

If you abide in Me, and My words abide in you, you will ask what you desire, and it shall be done for you.

JOHN 15:7

And in that day you will ask Me nothing. Most assuredly, I say to you, whatever you ask the Father in My name He will give you.

JOHN 16:23

Let us therefore come boldly to the throne of grace, that we may obtain mercy and find grace to help in time of need.

HEBREWS 4:16

Delight yourself also in the LORD,
   And He shall give you the desires of your heart.

PSALM 37:4

He shall call upon Me, and I will answer him;
   I will be with him in trouble;
   I will deliver him and honor him.

PSALM 91:15

Call to Me, and I will answer you, and show you great and mighty things, which you do not know.

JEREMIAH 33:3

But you, when you pray, go into your room, and when you have shut your door, pray to your Father who is in the secret place; and your Father who sees in secret will reward you openly.

MATTHEW 6:6

TRUTH FROM THE BIBLE ABOUT . . .

# UNSAVED LOVED ONES

So they said, "Believe on the Lord Jesus Christ, and you will be saved, you and your household."

ACTS 16:31

Who will tell you words by which you and all your household will be saved.

ACTS 11:14

For I will pour water on him who is thirsty,
    And floods on the dry ground;
    I will pour My Spirit on your descendants,
    And My blessing on your offspring.

ISAIAH 44:3

The Lord is not slack concerning His promise, as some count slackness, but is longsuffering toward us, not willing that any should perish but that all should come to repentance.

2 PETER 3:9

Wives, likewise, be submissive to your own husbands, that even if some do not obey the word, they, without a word, may be won by the conduct of their wives, when they observe your chaste conduct accompanied by fear.

1 PETER 3:1–2

And a woman who has a husband who does not believe, if he is willing to live with her, let her not divorce him. For the unbelieving husband is sanctified by the wife, and the unbelieving wife is sanctified by the husband; otherwise your children would be unclean, but now they are holy. But if the unbeliever departs, let him depart; a brother or a sister is not under bondage in such cases. But God has called us to peace. For how do you know, O wife, whether you will save your husband? Or how do you know, O husband, whether you will save your wife?

1 CORINTHIANS 7:13–16

Even so it is not the will of your Father who is in heaven that one of these little ones should perish.

MATTHEW 18:14

Who among you fears the LORD?
   Who obeys the voice of His Servant?
   Who walks in darkness
   And has no light?
   Let him trust in the name of the LORD
   And rely upon his God.

ISAIAH 50:10

Test all things; hold fast what is good. Abstain from every form of evil.

1 THESSALONIANS 5:21–22

The LORD has made known His salvation;
   His righteousness He has revealed in the sight of
      the nations.

PSALM 98:2

Cast your burden on the LORD,
   And He shall sustain you;
   He shall never permit the righteous to be moved.

PSALM 55:22

Thus says the LORD:

"Keep justice, and do righteousness,
For My salvation is about to come,
And My righteousness to be revealed."

ISAIAH 56:1

Nevertheless I tell you the truth. It is to your advantage that I go away; for if I do not go away, the Helper will not come to you; but if I depart, I will send Him to you. And when He has come, He will convict the world of sin, and of righteousness, and of judgment.

JOHN 16:7–8

Train up a child in the way he should go,
And when he is old he will not depart from it.

PROVERBS 22:6

He who calls you is faithful, who also will do it.

1 THESSALONIANS 5:24

# MARRIAGE

And the LORD God said, "It is not good that man should be alone; I will make him a helper comparable to him."

GENESIS 2:18

Therefore a man shall leave his father and mother and be joined to his wife, and they shall become one flesh.

GENESIS 2:24

He who finds a wife finds a good thing,
  And obtains favor from the LORD.

PROVERBS 18:22

Take wives and beget sons and daughters; and take wives for your sons and give your daughters to husbands, so that they may bear sons and daughters—that you may be increased there, and not diminished.

JEREMIAH 29:6

I will betroth you to Me forever;
   Yes, I will betroth you to Me
   In righteousness and justice,
   In lovingkindness and mercy;
   I will betroth you to Me in faithfulness,
   And you shall know the LORD.

HOSEA 2:19–20

Nevertheless, because of sexual immorality, let each man have his own wife, and let each woman have her own husband. Let the husband render to his wife the affection due her, and likewise also the wife to her husband. The wife does not have authority over her own body, but the husband does. And likewise the husband does not have authority over his own body, but the wife does.

1 CORINTHIANS 7:2–4

Therefore I desire that the younger widows marry, bear children, manage the house, give no opportunity to the adversary to speak reproachfully.

1 TIMOTHY 5:14

Husbands, love your wives, just as Christ also loved the church and gave Himself for her, that He might sanctify and cleanse her with the washing of water by the word, that He might present her to Himself a glorious church, not having spot or wrinkle or any such thing, but that she should be holy and without blemish. So husbands ought to love their own wives as their own bodies; he who loves his wife loves himself. For no one ever hated his own flesh, but nourishes and cherishes it, just as the Lord does the church. For we are members of His body, of His flesh and of His bones. "For this reason a man shall leave his father and mother and be joined to his wife, and the two shall become one flesh." This is a great mystery, but I speak concerning Christ and the church. Nevertheless let each one of you in particular so love his own wife as himself, and let the wife see that she respects her husband.

EPHESIANS 5:25–33

Marriage is honorable among all, and the bed undefiled; but fornicators and adulterers God will judge.

HEBREWS 13:4

Wives, likewise, be submissive to your own husbands, that even if some do not obey the word, they, without a word, may be won by the conduct of their wives.

1 PETER 3:1

Husbands, likewise, dwell with them with understanding, giving honor to the wife, as to the weaker vessel, and as being heirs together of the grace of life, that your prayers may not be hindered.

1 PETER 3:7

# DIVORCE

Furthermore it has been said, "Whoever divorces his wife, let him give her a certificate of divorce." But I say to you that whoever divorces his wife for any reason except sexual immorality causes her to commit adultery; and whoever marries a woman who is divorced commits adultery.

MATTHEW 5:31–32

"They say, 'If a man divorces his wife,
 And she goes from him
 And becomes another man's,
 May he return to her again?'
 Would not that land be greatly polluted?
 But you have played the harlot with many lovers;
 Yet return to Me," says the LORD.

JEREMIAH 3:1

The Pharisees came and asked Him, "Is it lawful for a man to divorce his wife?" testing Him.

And He answered and said to them, "What did Moses command you?"

They said, "Moses permitted a man to write a certificate of divorce, and to dismiss her."

And Jesus answered and said to them, "Because of the hardness of your heart he wrote you this precept. But from the beginning of the creation, God 'made them male and female.' 'For this reason a man shall leave his father and mother and be joined to his wife, and the two shall become one flesh'; so then they are no longer two, but one flesh. Therefore what God has joined together, let not man separate."

In the house His disciples also asked Him again about the same matter. So He said to them, "Whoever divorces his wife and marries another commits adultery against her. And if a woman divorces her husband and marries another, she commits adultery."

MARK 10:2–12

Now to the married I command, yet not I but the Lord: A wife is not to depart from her husband. But even if she does depart, let her remain unmarried or be reconciled to her husband. And a husband is not to divorce his wife.

But to the rest I, not the Lord, say: If any brother has a wife who does not believe, and she is willing to live with him, let him not divorce her. And a woman who has a husband who does not believe, if he is willing to live with her, let her not divorce him. For the unbelieving husband is sanctified by the wife, and the unbelieving wife is sanctified by the husband; otherwise your children would be unclean, but now they are holy. But if the unbeliever departs, let him depart; a brother or a sister is not under bondage in such cases. But God has called us to peace. For how do you know, O wife, whether you will save your husband? Or how do you know, O husband, whether you will save your wife?

But as God has distributed to each one, as the Lord has called each one, so let him walk. And so I ordain in all the churches.

1 CORINTHIANS 7:10–17

When a man takes a wife and marries her, and it happens that she finds no favor in his eyes because he has found some uncleanness in her, and he writes her a certificate of divorce, puts it in her hand, and sends her out of his house, when she has departed from his house, and goes and becomes another man's wife, if the latter husband detests her and writes her a certificate of divorce, puts it in her hand, and sends her out of his house, or if the latter husband dies who took her as his wife, then her former husband who divorced her must not take her back to be his wife after she has been defiled; for that is an abomination before the Lᴏʀᴅ, and you shall not bring sin on the land which the Lᴏʀᴅ your God is giving you as an inheritance.

DEUTERONOMY 24:1–4

# YOUR FAMILY

So they said, "Believe on the Lord Jesus Christ, and you will be saved, you and your household."

ACTS 16:31

And if it seems evil to you to serve the LORD, choose for yourselves this day whom you will serve, whether the gods which your fathers served that were on the other side of the River, or the gods of the Amorites, in whose land you dwell. But as for me and my house, we will serve the LORD.

JOSHUA 24:15

Train up a child in the way he should go,
    And when he is old he will not depart from it.

PROVERBS 22:6

Honor your father and your mother, that your days may be long upon the land which the LORD your God is giving you.

EXODUS 20:12

Let all bitterness, wrath, anger, clamor, and evil speaking be put away from you, with all malice. And be kind to one another, tenderhearted, forgiving one another, even as God in Christ forgave you.

EPHESIANS 4:31–32

One who rules his own house well, having his children in submission with all reverence (for if a man does not know how to rule his own house, how will he take care of the church of God?).

1 TIMOTHY 3:4–5

Behold, children are a heritage from the LORD,
The fruit of the womb is a reward.
Like arrows in the hand of a warrior,
So are the children of one's youth.
Happy is the man who has his quiver full of them;
They shall not be ashamed,
But shall speak with their enemies in the gate.

PSALM 127:3–5

Children's children are the crown of old men,
And the glory of children is their father.

PROVERBS 17:6

And he will turn
> The hearts of the fathers to the children,
> And the hearts of the children to their fathers,
> Lest I come and strike the earth with a curse.

MALACHI 4:6

And these words which I command you today shall be in your heart. You shall teach them diligently to your children, and shall talk of them when you sit in your house, when you walk by the way, when you lie down, and when you rise up. You shall bind them as a sign on your hand, and they shall be as frontlets between your eyes. You shall write them on the doorposts of your house and on your gates.

DEUTERONOMY 6:6–9

Correct your son, and he will give you rest;
> Yes, he will give delight to your soul.

PROVERBS 29:17

And you, fathers, do not provoke your children to wrath, but bring them up in the training and admonition of the Lord.

EPHESIANS 6:4

A good man leaves an inheritance to his children's
        children,
    But the wealth of the sinner is stored up for the
        righteous.

PROVERBS 13:22

Blessed is every one who fears the LORD,
    Who walks in His ways.
When you eat the labor of your hands,
    You shall be happy, and it shall be well with you.
    Your wife shall be like a fruitful vine
    In the very heart of your house,
    Your children like olive plants
    All around your table.
    Behold, thus shall the man be blessed
    Who fears the LORD.

PSALM 128:1–4

The father of the righteous will greatly rejoice,
    And he who begets a wise child will delight in him.

PROVERBS 23:24

TRUTH FROM THE BIBLE ABOUT . . .

# WIVES

He who finds a wife finds a good thing,
    And obtains favor from the LORD.

PROVERBS 18:22

Let the husband render to his wife the affection due
her, and likewise also the wife to her husband.

1 CORINTHIANS 7:3

Let your fountain be blessed,
    And rejoice with the wife of your youth.
    As a loving deer and a graceful doe,
    Let her breasts satisfy you at all times;
    And always be enraptured with her love.

PROVERBS 5:18–19

Your wife shall be like a fruitful vine
    In the very heart of your house,
    Your children like olive plants
    All around your table.

PSALM 128:3

Wives, submit to your own husbands, as is fitting in the Lord.

COLOSSIANS 3:18

Live joyfully with the wife whom you love all the days of your vain life which He has given you under the sun, all your days of vanity; for that is your portion in life, and in the labor which you perform under the sun.

ECCLESIASTES 9:9

An excellent wife is the crown of her husband,
But she who causes shame is like rottenness in his bones.

PROVERBS 12:4

The wise woman builds her house,
But the foolish pulls it down with her hands.

PROVERBS 14:1

Houses and riches are an inheritance from fathers,
But a prudent wife is from the LORD.

PROVERBS 19:14

Who can find a virtuous wife?
    For her worth is far above rubies.
    The heart of her husband safely trusts her;
    So he will have no lack of gain.
    She does him good and not evil
    All the days of her life.
    She seeks wool and flax,
    And willingly works with her hands.
    She is like the merchant ships,
    She brings her food from afar.
    She also rises while it is yet night,
    And provides food for her household,
    And a portion for her maidservants.
    She considers a field and buys it;
    From her profits she plants a vineyard.
    She girds herself with strength,
    And strengthens her arms.
    She perceives that her merchandise is good,
    And her lamp does not go out by night.
    She stretches out her hands to the distaff,
    And her hand holds the spindle.
    She extends her hand to the poor,
    Yes, she reaches out her hands to the needy.
    She is not afraid of snow for her household,

For all her household is clothed with scarlet.
She makes tapestry for herself;
Her clothing is fine linen and purple.
Her husband is known in the gates,
When he sits among the elders of the land.
She makes linen garments and sells them,
And supplies sashes for the merchants.
Strength and honor are her clothing;
She shall rejoice in time to come.
She opens her mouth with wisdom,
And on her tongue is the law of kindness.
She watches over the ways of her household,
And does not eat the bread of idleness.
Her children rise up and call her blessed;
Her husband also, and he praises her:
"Many daughters have done well,
But you excel them all."
Charm is deceitful and beauty is passing,
But a woman who fears the Lord, she shall be
      praised.
Give her of the fruit of her hands,
And let her own works praise her in the gates.

PROVERBS 31:10–31

TRUTH FROM THE BIBLE ABOUT . . .

# WIDOWS

Pure and undefiled religion before God and the Father is this: to visit orphans and widows in their trouble, and to keep oneself unspotted from the world.

JAMES 1:27

The blessing of a perishing man came upon me,
And I caused the widow's heart to sing for joy.

JOB 29:13

He administers justice for the fatherless and the widow, and loves the stranger, giving him food and clothing.

DEUTERONOMY 10:18

The LORD will destroy the house of the proud,
But He will establish the boundary of the widow.

PROVERBS 15:25

The Lord watches over the strangers;
He relieves the fatherless and widow;
But the way of the wicked He turns upside down.

PSALM 146:9

Leave your fatherless children,
I will preserve them alive;
And let your widows trust in Me.

JEREMIAH 49:11

For your Maker is your husband,
The Lord of hosts is His name;
And your Redeemer is the Holy One of Israel;
He is called the God of the whole earth.

ISAIAH 54:5

A wife is bound by law as long as her husband lives; but if her husband dies, she is at liberty to be married to whom she wishes, only in the Lord. But she is happier if she remains as she is, according to my judgment—and I think I also have the Spirit of God.

1 CORINTHIANS 7:39–40

He heals the brokenhearted
And binds up their wounds.

PSALM 147:3

A father of the fatherless, a defender of widows,
Is God in His holy habitation.

PSALM 68:5

I will not leave you orphans; I will come to you.

JOHN 14:18

"Cursed is the one who perverts the justice due the stranger, the fatherless, and widow."
And all the people shall say, "Amen!"

DEUTERONOMY 27:19

Therefore by Him let us continually offer the sacrifice of praise to God, that is, the fruit of our lips, giving thanks to His name.

HEBREWS 13:15

Teaching them to observe all things that I have commanded you; and lo, I am with you always, even to the end of the age. Amen.

MATTHEW 28:20

# SINGLES

I will betroth you to Me forever;
　　Yes, I will betroth you to Me
　　In righteousness and justice,
　　In lovingkindness and mercy.

HOSEA 2:19

But I say to the unmarried and to the widows: It is good for them if they remain even as I am.

1 CORINTHIANS 7:8

But as God has distributed to each one, as the Lord has called each one, so let him walk. And so I ordain in all the churches.

1 CORINTHIANS 7:17

Nevertheless he who stands steadfast in his heart, having no necessity, but has power over his own will, and has so determined in his heart that he will keep his virgin, does well.

1 CORINTHIANS 7:37

Are you bound to a wife? Do not seek to be loosed. Are you loosed from a wife? Do not seek a wife. But even if you do marry, you have not sinned; and if a virgin marries, she has not sinned. Nevertheless such will have trouble in the flesh, but I would spare you.

1 CORINTHIANS 7:27–28

But I want you to be without care. He who is unmarried cares for the things of the Lord—how he may please the Lord. But he who is married cares about the things of the world—how he may please his wife. . . . And this I say for your own profit, not that I may put a leash on you, but for what is proper, and that you may serve the Lord without distraction.

1 CORINTHIANS 7:32–33, 35

Marriage is honorable among all, and the bed undefiled; but fornicators and adulterers God will judge.

HEBREWS 13:4

But let each one examine his own work, and then he will have rejoicing in himself alone, and not in another.

GALATIANS 6:4

Trust in the LORD with all your heart,
And lean not on your own understanding;
In all your ways acknowledge Him,
And He shall direct your paths.

PROVERBS 3:5–6

Delight yourself also in the LORD,
And He shall give you the desires of your heart.

PSALM 37:4

Therefore, my brethren, you also have become dead to the law through the body of Christ, that you may be married to another—to Him who was raised from the dead, that we should bear fruit to God.

ROMANS 7:4

To knowledge self-control, to self-control perseverance, to perseverance godliness, to godliness brotherly kindness, and to brotherly kindness love. For if these things are yours and abound, you will be neither barren nor unfruitful in the knowledge of our Lord Jesus Christ.

2 PETER 1:6–8

TRUTH FROM THE BIBLE ABOUT . . .

# THE ELDERLY

Even to your old age, I am He,
    And even to gray hairs I will carry you!
    I have made, and I will bear;
    Even I will carry, and will deliver you.

                          ISAIAH 46:4

O God, You have taught me from my youth;
    And to this day I declare Your wondrous works.
    Now also when I am old and grayheaded,
    O God, do not forsake me,
    Until I declare your strength to this generation,
    Your power to everyone who is to come.

                      PSALM 71:17–18

Yea, though I walk through the valley of the shadow
        of death,
    I will fear no evil;
    For You are with me;
    Your rod and Your staff, they comfort me.

                      PSALM 23:4

The glory of young men is their strength,
  And the splendor of old men is their gray head.

PROVERBS 20:29

The silver-haired head is a crown of glory,
  If it is found in the way of righteousness.

PROVERBS 16:31

They shall still bear fruit in old age;
  They shall be fresh and flourishing.

PSALM 92:14

For length of days and long life
  And peace they will add to you.

PROVERBS 3:2

With long life I will satisfy him,
  And show him My salvation.

PSALM 91:16

I have been young, and now am old;
  Yet I have not seen the righteous forsaken,
  Nor his descendants begging bread.

PSALM 37:25

Let your conduct be without covetousness; be content with such things as you have. For He Himself has said, "I will never leave you nor forsake you."

HEBREWS 13:5

For what is our hope, or joy, or crown of rejoicing? Is it not even you in the presence of our Lord Jesus Christ at His coming?

1 THESSALONIANS 2:19

The poor and needy seek water, but there is none,
  Their tongues fail for thirst.
  I, the LORD, will hear them;
  I, the God of Israel, will not forsake them.

ISAIAH 41:17

For I am persuaded that neither death nor life, nor angels nor principalities nor powers, nor things present nor things to come, nor height nor depth, nor any other created thing, shall be able to separate us from the love of God which is in Christ Jesus our Lord.

ROMANS 8:38–39

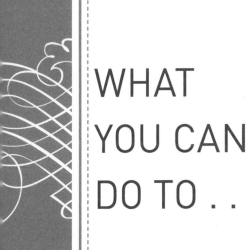

WHAT
YOU CAN
DO TO . . .

WHAT YOU CAN DO TO . . .

# GROW SPIRITUALLY

---

But grow in the grace and knowledge of our Lord and Savior Jesus Christ.

To Him be the glory both now and forever. Amen.

2 PETER 3:18

As newborn babes, desire the pure milk of the word, that you may grow thereby, if indeed you have tasted that the Lord is gracious.

1 PETER 2:2–3

But also for this very reason, giving all diligence, add to your faith virtue, to virtue knowledge, to knowledge self-control, to self-control perseverance, to perse-verance godliness, to godliness brotherly kindness, and to brotherly kindness love. For if these things are yours and abound, you will be neither barren nor unfruitful in the knowledge of our Lord Jesus Christ.

2 PETER 1:5–8

Be diligent to present yourself approved to God, a worker who does not need to be ashamed, rightly dividing the word of truth.

2 TIMOTHY 2:15

Meditate on these things; give yourself entirely to them, that your progress may be evident to all.

1 TIMOTHY 4:15

Therefore, leaving the discussion of the elementary principles of Christ, let us go on to perfection.

HEBREWS 6:1

For this reason we also, since the day we heard it, do not cease to pray for you, and to ask that you may be filled with the knowledge of His will in all wisdom and spiritual understanding; that you may walk worthy of the Lord, fully pleasing Him, being fruitful in every good work and increasing in the knowledge of God; strengthened with all might, according to His glorious power, for all patience and longsuffering with joy.

COLOSSIANS 1:9–11

For this reason I bow my knees to the Father of our Lord Jesus Christ, from whom the whole family in heaven and earth is named, that He would grant you, according to the riches of His glory, to be strengthened with might through His Spirit in the inner man, that Christ may dwell in your hearts through faith; that you, being rooted and grounded in love, may be able to comprehend with all the saints what is the width and length and depth and height—to know the love of Christ which passes knowledge; that you may be filled with all the fullness of God.

EPHESIANS 3:14–19

Let the word of Christ dwell in you richly in all wisdom, teaching and admonishing one another in psalms and hymns and spiritual songs, singing with grace in your hearts to the Lord.

COLOSSIANS 3:16

But we all, with unveiled face, beholding as in a mirror the glory of the Lord, are being transformed into the same image from glory to glory, just as by the Spirit of the Lord.

2 CORINTHIANS 3:18

The righteous shall flourish like a palm tree,
He shall grow like a cedar in Lebanon.

PSALM 92:12

Being confident of this very thing, that He who has begun a good work in you will complete it until the day of Jesus Christ. . . .

And this I pray, that your love may abound still more and more in knowledge and all discernment, that you may approve the things that are excellent, that you may be sincere and without offense till the day of Christ.

PHILIPPIANS 1:6, 9–10

That we should no longer be children, tossed to and fro and carried about with every wind of doctrine, by the trickery of men, in the cunning craftiness of deceitful plotting, but, speaking the truth in love, may grow up in all things into him who is the head—Christ.

EPHESIANS 4:14–15

WHAT YOU CAN DO TO . . .

# CHANGE THE WORLD

---

You are the light of the world. A city that is set on a hill cannot be hidden. Nor do they light a lamp and put it under a basket, but on a lampstand, and it gives light to all who are in the house. Let your light so shine before men, that they may see your good works and glorify your Father in heaven.

MATTHEW 5:14–16

Those who are wise shall shine
    Like the brightness of the firmament,
    And those who turn many to righteousness
    Like the stars forever and ever.

DANIEL 12:3

But you shall receive power when the Holy Spirit has come upon you; and you shall be witnesses to Me in Jerusalem, and in all Judea and Samaria, and to the end of the earth.

ACTS 1:8

And He said to them, "Go into all the world and preach the gospel to every creature. He who believes and is baptized will be saved; but he who does not believe will be condemned. And these signs will follow those who believe: In My name they will cast out demons; they will speak with new tongues; they will take up serpents; and if they drink anything deadly, it will by no means hurt them; they will lay hands on the sick, and they will recover."

So then, after the Lord had spoken to them, He was received up into heaven, and sat down at the right hand of God. And they went out and preached everywhere, the Lord working with them and confirming the word through the accompanying signs. Amen.

MARK 16:15–20

Go therefore and make disciples of all the nations, baptizing them in the name of the Father and of the Son and of the Holy Spirit, teaching them to observe all things that I have commanded you; and lo, I am with you always, even to the end of the age. Amen.

MATTHEW 28:19–20

The Spirit of the Lord is upon Me,
Because he has anointed Me
To preach the gospel to the poor;
He has sent Me to heal the brokenhearted,
To proclaim liberty to the captives
And recovery of sight to the blind,
To set at liberty those who are oppressed.

LUKE 4:18

And I also say to you that you are Peter, and on this rock I will build My church, and the gates of Hades shall not prevail against it. And I will give you the keys of the kingdom of heaven, and whatever you bind on earth will be bound in heaven, and whatever you loose on earth will be loosed in heaven.

MATTHEW 16:18–19

A new commandment I give to you, that you love one another; as I have loved you, that you also love one another. By this all will know that you are My disciples, if you have love for one another.

JOHN 13:34–35

Most assuredly, I say to you, he who believes in Me, the works that I do he will do also; and greater works than these he will do, because I go to My Father.

JOHN 14:12

We are of God. He who knows God hears us; he who is not of God does not hear us. By this we know the spirit of truth and the spirit of error. . . .

And we have known and believed the love that God has for us. God is love, and he who abides in love abides in God, and God in him.

Love has been perfected among us in this: that we may have boldness in the day of judgment; because as He is, so are we in this world.

1 JOHN 4:6, 16–17

For whatever is born of God overcomes the world. And this is the victory that has overcome the world— our faith. Who is he who overcomes the world, but he who believes that Jesus is the Son of God?

1 JOHN 5:4–5

WHAT YOU CAN DO TO . . .

# HELP YOUR BUSINESS

---

This Book of the Law shall not depart from your mouth, but you shall meditate in it day and night, that you may observe to do according to all that is written in it. For then you will make your way prosperous, and then you will have good success.

JOSHUA 1:8

Thus says the LORD, your Redeemer,
The Holy One of Israel:
"I am the LORD your God,
Who teaches you to profit,
Who leads you by the way you should go."

ISAIAH 48:17

Beloved, I pray that you may prosper in all things and be in health, just as your soul prospers.

3 JOHN V. 2

And you shall remember the L ORD your God, for it is He who gives you power to get wealth, that He may establish His covenant which He swore to your fathers, as it is this day.

DEUTERONOMY 8:18

Trust in the L ORD with all your heart,
And lean not on your own understanding;
In all your ways acknowledge Him,
And He shall direct your paths.
Do not be wise in your own eyes;
Fear the L ORD and depart from evil.
It will be health to your flesh,
And strength to your bones.
Honor the L ORD with your possessions,
And with the firstfruits of all your increase;
So your barns will be filled with plenty,
And your vats will overflow with new wine.

PROVERBS 3:5–10

If they obey and serve Him,
They shall spend their days in prosperity,
And their years in pleasures.

JOB 36:11

Then you will prosper, if you take care to fulfill the statutes and judgments with which the LORD charged Moses concerning Israel. Be strong and of good courage; do not fear nor be dismayed.

1 CHRONICLES 22:13

But seek first the kingdom of God and His righteousness, and all these things shall be added to you.

MATTHEW 6:33

Commit your works to the LORD,
    And your thoughts will be established.

PROVERBS 16:3

Through wisdom a house is built,
    And by understanding it is established;
    By knowledge the rooms are filled
    With all precious and pleasant riches.

PROVERBS 24:3–4

WHAT YOU CAN DO TO . . .

# PLEASE GOD

Everyone who is called by My name,
   Whom I have created for My glory;
   I have formed him, yes, I have made him. . . .
This people I have formed for Myself;
   They shall declare My praise.

ISAIAH 43:7, 21

But the hour is coming, and now is, when the true worshipers will worship the Father in spirit and truth; for the Father is seeking such to worship Him. God is Spirit, and those who worship Him must worship in spirit and truth.

JOHN 4:23–24

Therefore by Him let us continually offer the sacrifice of praise to God, that is, the fruit of our lips, giving thanks to His name. But do not forget to do good and to share, for with such sacrifices God is well pleased.

HEBREWS 13:15–16

Indeed it came to pass, when the trumpeters and singers were as one, to make one sound to be heard in praising and thanking the LORD, and when they lifted up their voice with the trumpets and cymbals and instruments of music, and praised the LORD, saying:

"For He is good,

For His mercy endures forever,"

that the house, the house of the LORD, was filled with a cloud, so that the priests could not continue ministering because of the cloud; for the glory of the LORD filled the house of God.

2 CHRONICLES 5:13–14

But without faith it is impossible to please Him, for he who comes to God must believe that He is, and that He is a rewarder of those who diligently seek Him.

HEBREWS 11:6

That you may walk worthy of the Lord, fully pleasing Him, being fruitful in every good work and increasing in the knowledge of God.

COLOSSIANS 1:10

You also, as living stones, are being built up a spiritual house, a holy priesthood, to offer up spiritual sacrifices acceptable to God through Jesus Christ. . . .

But you are a chosen generation, a royal priesthood, a holy nation, His own special people, that you may proclaim the praises of Him who called you out of darkness into His marvelous light.

1 PETER 2:5, 9

You are worthy, O Lord,
To receive glory and honor and power;
For You created all things,
And by Your will they exist and were created.

REVELATION 4:11

I beseech you therefore, brethren, by the mercies of God, that you present your bodies a living sacrifice, holy, acceptable to God, which is your reasonable service. And do not be conformed to this world, but be transformed by the renewing of your mind, that you may prove what is that good and acceptable and perfect will of God.

ROMANS 12:1–2

Therefore I exhort first of all that supplications, prayers, intercessions, and giving of thanks be made for all men. . . . For this is good and acceptable in the sight of God our Savior. . . .

I desire therefore that the men pray everywhere, lifting up holy hands, without wrath and doubting.

1 TIMOTHY 2:1, 3, 8

My mouth shall speak the praise of the LORD,
And all flesh shall bless His holy name
Forever and ever.

PSALM 145:21

And whatever we ask we receive from Him, because we keep His commandments and do those things that are pleasing in His sight.

1 JOHN 3:22

I will greatly praise the LORD with my mouth;
Yes, I will praise Him among the multitude.

PSALM 109:30

Oh, clap your hands, all you peoples!
Shout to God with the voice of triumph!

PSALM 47:1

The LORD takes pleasure in those who fear Him,
In those who hope in His mercy.

PSALM 147:11

So then, those who are in the flesh cannot please God.
But you are not in the flesh but in the Spirit.

ROMANS 8:8–9

# GOD'S
# PLAN OF
# SALVATION . . .

# GOD'S PLAN OF SALVATION

Therefore, just as through one man sin entered the world, and death through sin, and thus death spread to all men, because all sinned.

ROMANS 5:12

Moreover, brethren, I declare to you the gospel which I preached to you, which also you received and in which you stand, by which also you are saved, if you hold fast that word which I preached to you—unless you believed in vain.

For I delivered to you first of all that which I also received: that Christ died for our sins according to the Scriptures, and that He was buried, and that He rose again the third day according to the Scriptures.

1 CORINTHIANS 15:1–4

For the wages of sin is death, but the gift of God is eternal life in Christ Jesus our Lord.

ROMANS 6:23

But God demonstrates His own love toward us, in that while we were still sinners, Christ died for us.

ROMANS 5:8

For God did not send His Son into the world to condemn the world, but that the world through Him might be saved.

JOHN 3:17

He who believes in the Son has everlasting life; and he who does not believe the Son shall not see life, but the wrath of God abides on him.

JOHN 3:36

For God so loved the world that He gave His only begotten Son, that whoever believes in Him should not perish but have everlasting life.

JOHN 3:16

But as many as received Him, to them He gave the right to become children of God, to those who believe in His name.

JOHN 1:12

For by grace you have been saved through faith, and that not of yourselves; it is the gift of God, not of works, lest anyone should boast.

EPHESIANS 2:8–9

Behold, I stand at the door and knock. If anyone hears My voice and opens the door, I will come in to him and dine with him, and he with Me.

REVELATION 3:20

Therefore whoever confesses Me before men, him I will also confess before My Father who is in heaven.

MATTHEW 10:32

# NOTES

# NOTES

# NOTES

# NOTES